Understanding

and Maximizing

the

Gifts of

Prophecy

Volume 1

By

Dr. Levy Q. Barnes, Jr.

Copyright © 2017 by Dr. Levy Q. Barnes, Jr prelate

ISBN 978-1-365-89183-0

Library of Congress Cataloging in Publication Data

Barnes, Levy

Understanding and Maximizing the Gifts of Prophecy

Volume 1

Acknowledgments

First, I would like to give thanks to my best friend, Jesus Christ, for teaching and bringing out the best in me. Next, I'd like to thank my beautiful wife, Sheri Barnes. You inspire me to do greater things. I am also grateful for my two amazing sons—Levy III and Zachary. You are the best gifts God ever gave to me. I would like to thank my father and mother, Minister Levy Q. Barnes, Sr. and Dr. Vanessa Landry-Barnes prelate. Mom, you taught me to seek Jesus and love His people. You gave me my foundation in the learning of Jesus. Dad, you taught me to be independent. You also taught me how to create opportunities. Also, I'd like to appreciate my stepmom, Darnella Barnes, who also inspired me to inspire others. I would also like to thank my Granny, Dr. Marlene Thompson. You taught me to think outside of the box. Also, Grandmother Brenda Barnes and my grandpa, the late Levy Barnes; I love you so much. Thank you for always being proud of me and going the extra mile to see me rise. Also to my amazing siblings—Alii, Aulani, and Alakai, I love you, and I am so proud to hear you speak of your relationships with Jesus.

There are many others who have inspired and lifted me up. To my amazing godparents, Missionary Olivia Cooper and Karry Causey; you inspire me to strive for the greater. Thank you for your support with all of my projects. Thank you for believing in me. My gratitude also goes to my favorite uncle in the world, Wayne Landry. I love and appreciate you for pushing me to think bigger, dress my best, and ride looking fresh. To all of my aunts who have supported me including Elaine Thompson (and Uncle Jay), Dr. Theada Thompson, Rose Landry, Gaynelle Lofton (and family) and all of my aunts who have shown me love and support through the years, thank you. To the late Rev. Dr. Norwood Thompson, thank you for believing in my talents. Thank you, my awesome cousin and big brother, Ezra Landry. I love you and appreciate you for believing in me. To my amazing cousins—Elder Evangeline and Minister Andre Antoine, thank you. I love the two of you, and seeing you grow and evolve is a blessing to my heart. To my extended family, the amazing McCormicks, thank you for your talent, support, and inspiration. Danatus King Jr., I appreciate you for always being my best friend. Last but not least, I thank all my in-laws—Minister Isaiah Porter, Patricia Porter, Desmoine Porter (and family), Tyrone Porter (and family), Ivan Porter and Vaun Porter. I love all of you and thank you for your support through the years.

Also, special thanks to those who are not related to me but inspired me. Bishop Joseph Walker, you helped me to start on my philosophical journey by opening my understanding of the history of the Bible, not just the religion. Pastor Benny Hinn, you taught me how to make the Bible come alive and hear Jesus through every word I read. Ms. Diana K. Poe, you brought the voice out of me. You pushed me to my vocal limits, and I love you for that. To the late Bishop Eloise Marcel, you lead by example of how to be radical for Christ Jesus. Pastor Cynthia Williams, you lead by example on how to seek Jesus for everyone and reveal the truth of Jesus Christ.

Thanks to everyone who has been a part of my life. I send my love to all my comrades in the Gospel of Christ. We will spread the message of Jesus everywhere. So many people keep coming to my mind. If I were to thank everyone, I might have to write another book. But thank you. I love all of you.

Dedication

I dedicate this book to Jesus. He gave this to me during our secret times, so I dedicate it back to Him.

Table of Contents

Chapters

Preface

Understanding and Maximizing the Gifts of Prophecy

The gift of prophecy is a very radical gift, and it is often misused, misunderstood, and underused. This is a real gift and the best. No Christian should not believe that this gift isn't real because it is. There are so many different unique gifts of prophecy, and there are many ways to prophesy. Ultimately, prophecy is the testimony of Jesus (Revelation 19:10). Anything that deviates from Jesus Christ is not prophecy and could be something to stray believers away from God's ultimate divine path for their lives.

Many people see the glorious aspects of prophecy, but they do not understand the work, time, sacrifice, dedication, and responsibilities that are on us. It takes a lot of studying, praying, and spending time with God to master your prophetic gift or else; you can lead God's people astray. It also requires discipline to properly minister using prophecy. Prophets are human, and they make mistakes. In order for us to keep God's treasure safe, we must keep away from error.

Unfortunately, many people shun the spiritual gifts. Some people don't understand the gift of prophecy. There are even people who have been misled or abused by the gift of prophecy because someone mishandled them. When people have been offended by something, it is harder to win them over than a fortified city (Proverbs 18:19). I also was victimized by this gift because of someone operating in error. If it wasn't for me having the gift of prophecy and having a close relationship with Jesus, I could've been led astray.

With all of this being said, it leads me to tell you one of the ultimate reasons I'm writing this book. So many people go running wildly when they hear someone is a prophet. They want to see miraculous things, and rightfully so. We want to see proof that Jesus is still moving. Jesus promises us signs and wonders (Mark 16:17-18). As a prophet, the Word of God comes from God and then goes through the man or woman who is representing Him. There are some people who, unintentionally, misrepresent God and infiltrate their own beliefs along with what God has spoken. Because I was mishandled, I had to learn how to get the information I needed from God instead of getting it from God through a prophet. This way, I was able to get a clear unpolluted word from God. Then God showed me that it is possible for anyone to prophesy and operate in the prophetic gifts (1 Corinthians 14:5 and 1 Corinthians 14:39-40).

Anyone can obtain the prophetic gift, but they must be willing to go to the extreme. I believe that those who are reading this book are willing to go to the extreme for Jesus. You must have a strong desire to be with Jesus in order to operate in spiritual gifts like prophecy. Our faith must go to another plateau because the world and life of a prophet seem fictitious to the world. Some people who may read this book centuries from now may think of this as being a book of fairy tales, but in the world of a prophet, these things happen every day.

If you are ready to go where God has graced me, then proceed to read past this point. I am now removing all filters, and I will allow God to speak directly. Through the series of these books, God will walk with you through His Word and show how to use the gifts of prophecy to: cast out devils, heal the sick, see into the past, see in the spirit, discern, see into the future, control nature, control the weather, break curses, send curses, understand mysteries, rebuke death, create life, and understand Jesus in a way you never have.

Note: As you read this, if you plan on cross-referencing with your Bible, you will need a King James Version Bible. Some of the newer translations verbiages are inaccurate, and certain mysteries were lost due to the language being modernized. To fully comprehend each referenced scripture, I suggest you use a King James Version. This is not to discredit any other versions, and you are welcome to use them. I would like for you to get a full comprehension of everything that is stated in this book.

Chapter 1

What is Prophecy?

According to the dictionary, prophecy is foretelling the future. According to scripture, prophecy embodies this definition as well, but ultimately, prophecy is the testimony of Jesus Christ (Revelation 19:10). Prophecy is a spiritual gift (1 Corinthians 12:10). With the gift comes the ability to do many things. If you consider fire a gift, you must realize that it can do many things. Fire can warm your body, heat up your food, burn matter to ashes, change the composition of matter, manipulate water, and many other things. The same thing falls with the gift of prophecy. When you are using the gift of prophecy through Jesus Christ, you can see future events, see past events, understand how someone needs to obtain healing, cast out demons, control weather, control animals, visit with God, and many other things. Using the gift of prophecy without the component of Jesus Christ is not prophecy. This gift is utilized to ensure that the body of believers is aware of the activity of God so that we can be in His will.

Where do they originate?

The gift of prophecy is the second gift given to man, the first being miracles. Man originally had perfect communion with God, and we were in sync with God and the earth. When man fell from grace, God gave Adam and Eve their first set of curses and the first prophecies (Genesis 3:14-24). Because man fell from grace, this gift was provided to him to keep him aware of God's plans. As a reminder, ultimately, the spirit of prophecy is the testimony of Jesus Christ. The first prophecy is of Jesus Christ (Genesis 3:15).

What do they do?

Prophets usually arrive when evil rises. "When the enemy comes in like a flood, the Lord will raise up a standard against him" (Isaiah 59:19). Throughout scripture, when there was evil on the rise, a prophet would show up. The children of Israel were in slavery 400 years, and the Lord raised up Moses (Exodus 2-3). When the king of Mesopotamia enslaved them, the Lord raised up prophetic judges (Judges 3:9, 3:18, 4:1, 6:11, etc.). When David sinned with Bathsheba and against Uriah, God sent Nathan to correct him. When Ahab married Jezebel and caused Israel to sin, almost from nowhere, Elijah appears (1 Kings 17:1). Even before Jesus showed up, there was evil in the land. John the Baptist shows up coming out of the wilderness, preparing the way for Jesus. God sends prophets just in time. They are the ones who can defeat evil.

This isn't the only time prophets show up. They are present to represent God's voice on the earth. If a person is not directly linked to God or if God doesn't choose to make an appearance to them, He will use a prophet. For those who are already linked to God, He will speak to them or send an angel. Throughout the Bible, angels would only appear and send messages to believers. Everyone else received a preacher or a prophet (Genesis 22:11, Exodus 3:2, Daniel 10, Matthew 2:2 and 13, Luke 1:11 and 2:9). An excellent example of this is the wise men and the shepherds. The wise men learned of Jesus from His star. Some theologians say they understood astrology. An angel visited the Jewish shepherds. The shepherds saw Jesus as a baby, but the wise men didn't see Jesus until he was about two years old. This is not restricted to dreams and visions. God can show ungodly men and women dreams and visions. The only difference is that they will not understand the dreams and visions unless a Godly man or woman rises to accurately interpret it.

Prophets come to issue truth. When the ungodly see visions and dreams, the only one that can reveal the truth is Jesus Christ through the prophet. Pharaoh had a dream from God, and no one could interpret it because, among pharaoh's counselors, no one was connected to God. So, for the king to understand, He had to raise up Joseph to interpret the dream (Genesis 41). King Nebuchadnezzar had a dream and no one, but the prophet Daniel could interpret it (Daniel 2:34-45). He also interpreted the writing on the wall for King Belshazzar. Prophets come to reveal truth. Jesus' word is truth (John 17:17). So, when there are mysteries, dreams, or visions given, the prophet may be the only one who has the answer to reveal its message.

Chapter 2

Attaining the gift

How does someone become a prophet? This spiritual gift is one of the best gifts. People travel near and far to get a word of prophecy. I remember when I was in college, students would call me up for a prophetic word. At that time in my life, I had plenty of time to minister. Even the administrative staff workers and college professors would approach me for a prophetic word. When they would see the word of Jesus happen, they kept coming back, and they would regularly call me just to get a prophetic word. I thought to myself, the same way God speaks to me, I am sure He can speak to them. I understood that everyone wasn't born with the gift of prophecy, but I knew that just because they weren't born with it didn't mean that God wouldn't speak to them. So, I began to seek God on how others can obtain the gift of prophecy. After going through the Word of God, I realized that if someone desires God and the ability to prophesy, they can obtain the gift of prophecy. Paul the Apostle said that he wished that everyone spoke in tongues, but he rather that they prophesied. He also said we should covet the best gifts. This is proof that the gift can be attained even if they do not attain it at birth or their initial call to the ministry.

Ways to obtain the gift

BIRTH

Some people are born with the gift. Even before salvation, they may have dreams and visions of spiritual beings. Phillip happened to have four daughters who were prophetesses (Acts 21:9). The priestly mantle was passed down from generation to generation (Numbers 3:3). David and his son, Solomon, had prophetic gifts. In my family, my grandmother, mother, and I, operate in prophetic gifts. But the gift of prophecy is more contagious than just being hereditary.

Before I began to seek God the way I do now, I would have prophetic dreams. It started as a toddler. I would see demons and images that no child should see. My mother then taught me how to overcome Satan by Jesus at the age of four. In my dreams, demons would tie me down and try to do sacrilegious things to me and ultimately, sacrifice my body to an antichristian being. The night my mother taught me how to fight the devil through Jesus Christ, I had the first memory of a regular dream. The next night, I began to have dreams of end time events. I was sitting in my room looking out of the window seeing the world being destroyed by fire and Jesus was next to me and told me that was His will.

From that time to the time I began to seek Jesus the way I do now, I would have so many prophetic dreams that I would sometimes get what happened in real life mixed up with dreams that God showed me. I would have dreams of major catastrophes like Hurricane Katrina and the events that occurred in New York on 9/11, and it would just amaze me that God would allow me to see these things. When my father had his last son, God showed me the dream of it, and

I spoke with him about it the next week as if someone had the conversation with me about it. At the time, he lived in California, and I lived in Louisiana. I forgot I dreamed about it. He asked me, "How did I know his wife was pregnant with a boy?" He nor his wife told anyone of her being pregnant. I then remembered that God revealed it in a dream to me and I realized that no one told me. When I began to seek Jesus more deeply, I was able to understand why I'd have these dreams and how to utilize this information in ministry efficiently.

God speaks in many ways. God may talk to someone in a dream at night. Someone else may see an open vision while they are awake. Others may hear God speak in a still small voice. God can give someone discernment to understand which actions they need to take based on what they see in the spirit realm. God also speaks of events that happen in our lives. If He wants to use roaches in your kitchen to get a point to you, He will use it. He can use anything to speak to us, but are we watching and listening?

I have experienced prophets who can see your past and present phenomenally, and they will tell you that they don't even study the word of God. I've seen prophets have the ability to even know a person's name without even meeting them prior to it. I have also seen prophets know the medical history of a person without even knowing them. Yet, in order to effectively receive the full benefits of God, the prophet's life has to be pure. When it is pure, they are able to tie the past and present to get you a promising future through Jesus.

As mentioned earlier, not everyone is born with the gift. Also, not everyone has a random encounter with God singling you out from others. This is what differentiates you out from regular people. Some people desire spiritual gifts and don't have access to it. There is good news for you. Spiritual gifts can be attained.

As I mentioned earlier, I was a dreamer, and God blessed me with the gift of the Word of Wisdom (1 Corinthians 12:8) as a child after salvation. When I was in my 20s, I began to desire more of God. I wanted the gifts of tongues, then the gift of discernment of spirits, a stronger gift of prophecy, and the gift of healing. God revealed to me, through the Apostle Paul, that gifts can be attained (1 Corinthians 12:31, 14:1). Paul said to desire the best gifts and covet prophecy. Why would he ask us to do such a thing? The reason is that the gifts can be attained.

Several powerful gifts can be used in the spiritual, which in turn, affects the natural realm. We don't battle against flesh and blood, but against principalities and powers, spiritual wickedness in high places. This means spirits affect flesh and blood. Then flesh and blood can impact matter, homes, cars, jobs, etc. Therefore, spirits exert influence on everything. The only way to affect spirits is with spiritual gifts. The spiritual gifts include gifts of discernment of spirits, prophecy, healing, miracles, faith, the word of knowledge, the word of wisdom, tongues, and the interpretation of tongues. All of these gifts can be acquired if you desire to attain them.

The gift of the discernment of spirits allows you to be able to detect spiritual activity, detect people who are operating with certain spirits, and even detect spiritual beings whether they are good or bad. With this gift comes an extreme amount of love. I asked God for this gift after I received the gift of tongues when I was 21. I used to be so gullible. Someone could tell me the sky was yellow with a convincing argument and I'd believe them. They could tell me my laces were untied while I was wearing flip-flops, and

I'd go down to tie them. But all jokes aside, I was completely unaware of the spiritual activity around me.

I asked God for this gift of discernment of spirits, and I received an amazing amount of love for people almost immediately. I didn't understand why, but I just loved everyone I encountered. God, later on, explained to me why. With the gift of discernment, you see a person for who they are and what they are capable of. You may see something that is easy to judge and condemn them on. You may see that they possibly committed terrible crimes or heinous sins. You must minister to them with love. You cannot condemn them. I remember when I came across a man who was a child molester and rapist. Naturally, most people would send them underneath the prison. I had to minister to this man. If I didn't have the love from God, I might not have given the Word that God had for him.

I go into the streets and minister from time to time. I am very sensitive to smells. Anyone who knows me knows that I like cologne and I love fresh scents. People who are on the streets don't always have access to peppermints, gum, cologne, or maybe even soap. There were times when I smelled people I wanted to throw up, but in order to minister to them, love stepped in, and my throw-up feeling had to go another way because I saw a soul created by God. There were times I had to hug them and share the love of God with them in order to effectively minister the word of God.

I had to minister to alcoholics, drug addicts, rapists, pedophiles, homosexuals, lesbians, thieves, liars, murderers, adulterers, and many other people living in sin. When God gave me discernment, I would see it sometimes before I met them. There was a man who had HIV that I ministered to. Most traditional believers would say that was judgment for living life as a homosexual. Yet, even though it may have been his punishment for living in homosexuality, it wasn't my job to put him in the grave and judge him. He was God's creation that deserved love. I ministered Jesus Christ to my best and loved him with the love of Jesus. When you are moved with compassion, you can minister Jesus at your best. The last time I spoke with him, his HIV was undetectable. You understand that people make mistakes, but Jesus is able to transcend them from their past mistakes and make them a new person.

With the gift of discernment of spirits, you even have the ability to speak to spirits. It is important to talk with spirits when utilizing this gift. When I say talk to spirits, I don't mean we should have a friendly conversation. As a man or woman of God, we command these beings and curse them. When you have a friendly conversation, you are making a mistake, and this can easily turn into witchcraft. Adam and Eve made a mistake by having the wrong type of discussion with Satan. Remember, you MUST HAVE A CONVERSATION WITH SPIRITS, but you have power through Jesus Christ to defeat them.

When Adam and Eve had a conversation with the serpent, they entertained what he had to say. When Jesus had a conversation with demons, He commanded them and defeated them (Gen 3, Mark 5:6-8, Luke 8:28-31). When Adam and Eve had a conversation with the serpent, he convinced them of doing wrong. When Jesus had a conversation with Satan in the wilderness, He told him that he would not do wrong. The proper discussion for Adam and Eve would've been to dismiss the serpent and tell him that they would not eat of the fruit of the forbidden tree. When we encounter someone with a spirit or a being with a spirit in them, the conversation should usually go like this: *I am an ambassador for Jesus Christ, and I have power over unclean spirits. God has given me the power to trample over you. Get out of this person, and I curse you to be bound to hell in Jesus' name.*

The gift of prophecy is the first spiritual gift that was given to us. When Adam and Eve fell from grace, they needed something to keep them linked to God. Man initially had a divine connection to God. They would commune with God as He walked through the Garden of Eden with them. When they ate of the Tree of Knowledge of Good and Evil, they lost that link and began to hide from His Voice (Genesis 3:8). So, from that point, they needed a gift that would keep them informed of the moves that God would make.

The gift of prophecy is not just seeing in the past or seeing in the future. The gift of prophecy is a gift that alters the reality of most people. Let's think about it. People talking to animals is unheard of, but several times in scripture, prophets do communicate with animals (Genesis 3, Numbers 22:25-31). People being able to control the weather is something that is put in comic books, but there are scriptures where prophets controlled rain, fire, and even wind throughout the word of God. Being able to prophecy is amazing, yet it comes at a cost.

The ultimate gift of prophecy is the testimony of Jesus. Whenever you see the Voice of God, the Word of God, or the hand of God, it is referring to Jesus. John 1:1-14 says, "In the beginning was the Word and the Word was with God and the Word was God. The same was in the beginning with God." Then it says, "And the Word became flesh." This was Jesus. Even in the beginning of the Bible, the word was Jesus.

So, prophecy is a gift that connects us to Jesus. Prophets had the ability to change the weather, command animals, see the past, and see the future. Prophets alter the present reality. Prophets have a hard job though. Most of the time, people don't want to listen to what God is saying. Another thing is that we have to stay connected to Jesus in a mighty way or our gift can be perverted. Prophecy is considered the best gift (1 Corinthians 12:31).

The next gift is the gift of healing. All sicknesses can be healed through Jesus. There are recorded miracles. People have had limbs regrow, diseases healed, and life restored back to them. Many believers don't believe in healing anymore. Because of the lack of faith, many shy away from this gift. Even Jesus wasn't able to heal certain people because of their unbelief (Matthew 13:58, Mark 6:5). If you can build someone's faith up, Jesus can heal them through your hands.

I've been in services and through our ministry, the Lord has healed individuals that were bound to wheelchairs, and blind people regained sight. Yet, there have been services where people were not healed. I could even tell when I would approach a person, if they desired healing or not. Some individuals have become content with their illness. It's understandable. Many have to cope with the idea that they will be sick. But there are those who are willing to believe there is hope for their condition through Jesus Christ. There are individuals who have been healed through our ministry that weren't saved before we met them. But they were willing to believe in someone who could change their situation after the Gospel was presented.

A perfect example of this is two different women I ministered to in two different cities. One lady was pronounced legally blind. She was making preparations to be fully blind by going to blind classes that taught people how to cope with blindness, survive, and do basic tasks while being blind. She was a blessing to my ministry, so I prayed for her eyes and gave her instructions to start reading her Bible. I said that God would restore her eyes. The doctors told her that she didn't have long before she would not be able to see anything at all. Seven years later, I text her pictures of my wife and kids, and she's seeing everything I send her, and she can read my messages. The second woman was also blind. She didn't have enough faith to desire it. Some people enjoy illnesses as a crutch. I ministered to her, and as I prayed with her, God started opening her eyes. As we prayed, she screamed because she started seeing beams of light and was able to start seeing the formation of people. Her eyes then took focus, and she looked up at me and screamed. I knew I wasn't that bad looking for her to scream, but she was so startled because she was able to see me standing in front of her. I gave her instructions to do at home. She ended up going home, and the fear of losing disability shied her away from wanting complete healing. I saw her the next year, and she was worse off than before. I inquired of God, why? God said her faith wasn't strong enough to sustain her healing after she left service. When seeds are given, not all of it lands on the fruitful ground (Matthew 13).

The gifts of healing can alter a person's life. All diseases can be healed. The gift of healing gives you the ability to alter sicknesses. God can heal all things.

Another gift is the gift of miracles. Some people have this gift to cause the most miraculous things to happen. Like the gift of prophecy, the gift of miracles can alter reality.

Another gift is the gift of faith (1 Corinthians 12:8). When I met my wife, she didn't operate in the gift of prophecy or tongues. She had the spiritual gift of faith. She could believe something, and it would come to pass. This is not just having faith. This is the ability to believe things into existence.

Let's talk about the gift of the word of wisdom (1 Corinthians 12:8). As I mentioned earlier, the original gift that I was blessed with at salvation was the gift of the word of wisdom. This is the ability to have heavenly wisdom on subjects that you didn't even study. Don't misunderstand me. I do study. We must study to show ourselves approved. I had the ability to hear one thing, subject, or even a verse and have a complete understanding of it. When I look back at myself utilizing this gift, it simply amazes me. As a six-year-old kid, I would teach about Revelations to other kids and adults at the playground. While we would run around acting like animals, I would start a conversation about Jesus and start teaching from prophetic books to other kids who didn't know about Jesus. I would read one scripture sometimes and get the applicable wisdom for the entire book. I was twelve sitting in a classroom full of bishops. The teacher asked questions, and the upcoming bishops couldn't answer. I eventually broke the silence and started answering the questions. The teacher and the bishop elects were amazed. I became an ordained bishop by the age of 26 because of that gift. Even in my business endeavors, when the Holy Ghost prompts me, I receive wisdom in particular areas that surprise people in my profession that have been in my field for decades. It's through the Holy Ghost. The reason I am actually writing this book is not that I am such a great prophet. The reason is that since I have accessed the prophetic ability, I am able to use wisdom to teach on the gift.

The next gift we will talk about is the word of knowledge. The gift of the word of knowledge gives you the ability to access information that you shouldn't know. It can come as a simple word or information that will come to you as you minister. There was a prophet that I knew that operated in the gift of the word of knowledge. While ministering to individuals, God would drop a word of knowledge that he shouldn't have known about their past and apply the correction that needed to be made in the present. If you have the gift of the word of knowledge, you can have information to battle in the spirit realm and minister promise in the natural realm.

Another popular gift is the gift of tongues (1 Corinthians 12:10). The gift of tongues allows us to be able to communicate better with God. It is the ability to speak in other languages. These languages include languages of other nationalities and angels. (Acts 2:4-11, 1 Corinthians 13:1). This brings us closer to God and allows us to be edified (1 Corinthians 14:4). We have a stronger link to God in communication. We may not understand what we are saying, but God does. Our spirit is communicating with Him. When people speak in tongues, one of two things occur. The Holy Ghost is either making intercession for you, or the person who is speaking in tongues is speaking the wonders of God (Romans 8:26, Acts 2:11). Contrary to popular belief, when individuals speak in tongues, revelations are being given. The only way to find out what those revelations are is by having an interpreter.

The previous paragraph leads me to talk about the next gift that accompanies tongues which is the gift of the interpretation of tongues. The interpretation of tongues allows us to hear what is being said from the one that is speaking in tongues. I asked God for this gift ten years ago. I will never forget when God opened my ears to hear what someone was saying in their spiritual tongue. After I heard the man speak in his spiritual tongue, I approached him after the service and told him what he said. He was amazed because that was what he was recently praying for. Paul suggested that when someone spoke openly in tongues, there should be an interpreter. When they speak in tongues, it only edifies themselves. If an interpreter is present, the church can be edified (1 Corinthians 14:4).

COVETING

God forbade us to covet, but for us to attain spiritual gifts, He requires us to covet. We do not covet earthly things. We must set our affections on things above (Colossians 3:2). When someone is jealous, they may be willing to do whatever it takes to attain what they are coveting after. People had murdered, sacrificed, and done extraordinary things when they were jealous enough for earthly things including money, possessions, and even spouses. If you covet a spiritual gift, you will be willing to do whatever is required to attain it. If it means that you fast or pray longer, you are eager to go the extra mile. You must be willing to do this if you desire spiritual gifts.

ASKING

If you aren't born with a particular spiritual gift or if you don't receive a certain gift at salvation, there are several ways to attain other spiritual gifts. The first thing to do is simply ask. One of the easiest gifts to acquire is wisdom. Unfortunately, not many people ask God for that gift. Most people think that they already know everything they need to know. They usually don't know what they are missing. God freely gives out wisdom and doesn't take it back (Proverbs 2:6, James 1:5). We must first ask God for a spiritual gift.

EXTREMITY

Be ready to go to the extreme to attain and operate in certain spiritual gifts. We must be willing to sacrifice. There are times when God may have us to sacrifice food (1 Kings 13). God told a prophet to go to Bethel and prophecy against the temple. He told the prophet not to eat or drink. Some people can't even give up dessert. We must be prepared to sacrifice and go to the extreme if we want to operate in the spirit realm. The same prophet that came to Judah utilized his prophetic gift. As he cried, the altar turned into ashes. His gift was moving so strong that the king stretched his hand against the prophet and it dried up. This same prophet was killed simply because he didn't follow God's exact instructions.

If you desire more spiritual gifts, you must be willing to do whatever you have to do to follow God. You may have to give up certain people. Elisha received a mantle to be a prophet. He didn't even get to tell his family goodbye before he started his mission. You must be willing to forsake all. He could've missed a powerful calling, but he was willing to sacrifice. Ezekiel had to eat feces baked with bread because of a command that God gave (Ezekiel 4:15). We may have to give up food, people, behaviors, attitudes, possessions, and even careers in order to follow after God to attain spiritual gifts. The disciples had to leave their families to fulfill the work of Jesus when they followed Him. Are you willing to do the extreme?

When I began to seek God for more spiritual gifts, I fasted a lot. After I would end a fast, God would sometimes place me on another fast right after it. I would wake up early in the morning just to seek Jesus even if I went to sleep late. I wouldn't listen or watch certain things so that I could get clarity and hear from God. I was willing to do whatever I had to do to get His attention. By this time, I already was a dreamer and operated in the gift of the word of wisdom, but I wanted more from God.

I was part of a denomination that believed that if you didn't speak in tongues, you weren't saved and you didn't have the Holy Ghost. God didn't allow me to obtain the gift of tongues for many years after salvation. So, I thought was not saved and that I didn't have the Holy Ghost because of this. I was wrong and I am so glad that God prevented me from having that gift for many years so that I could attain a better understanding of how His spirit worked. I was born with the gift of prophecy and received the gift of the word of wisdom at salvation. It wasn't until I began to seek God in a more desperate way that I began attaining other gifts. I just simply asked God for the gifts in accompaniment with prayer, fasting, and going out of my way to get God's attention. I was saved, and I had the Holy Ghost, but I didn't have the gift that I was surrounded with at my church. Just because you don't speak in tongues doesn't mean you are not saved. If you are saved and belong to God, He may have given you a different spiritual gift. Everyone doesn't immediately identify the gift at salvation, but they have it, and they are using it.

ASSOCIATION

Another way to attain spiritual gifts is by association. Before I met my wife, she said she didn't dream of things that became a reality. After we courted for a month or so, she began having dreams of future events. It started off with her dreaming the way I was going to propose to her. I already made up in my mind when and how I was going to propose to her a month and a half after I met her. I knew she was going to be my wife and I wanted her as my wife, so I bought the ring and hid it a month and a half after I met her. I wanted to wait until New Year's when we would go to Dallas, TX. I wanted to introduce her to the last and one of the most important people in my family, which was my grandfather before I proposed. I wanted to go through the formalities of us meeting all of the important people in our families. She dreamed that she was proposed to when fireworks were going off. I planned to propose to her as soon as New Year's hit and fireworks were going off. I did just that. From that point on, she would have different dreams that would come to reality. My gift rubbed off on her.

Some gifts can almost be contagious. God has to ordain it first. Saul was on his way back to his father's house and came among prophets and began to prophesy among them. He was not a prophet, but the ordination that God had on his life in addition to the association he made brought the gift to manifestation (1 Samuel 10:11). You can be around someone who operates in specific anointings and sometimes, you can tap into it if you desire.

We may need to get around others in order to cultivate and master the gift. I feel that it is crucial for ministers of the Gospel to get appropriate training, education, and mentorship to fulfill their callings. Many individuals shy away from this. The moment they hear from God, they want to step out untrained. I will say that the majority of my knowledge in Christ came from Christ. Yet, I got my appropriate credentials so that I would not be a novice in my calling. I aimed at attaining as much training as possible before I launched out. Some of the training that I had helped me to understand better the information that Jesus shared with me along with the scriptures.

Even though I encourage getting training, ministry school, and being mentored, there's no comparison to the training that God can give. Moses did not go through ministry training, but he received his information directly from God (Exodus 3). God trained him on miracles and shared even historical information with him. Natural training can only do so much. You must get the rest directly from the source which is Jesus.

CHARACTER/GOD CALLING YOU OUT

Another way to receive a spiritual gift is when God calls you out. This can be beyond our control. God sees our characters and hearts and chooses to use us like He did Abraham, Moses, Mary, Paul, and several other Christian figures.

Other gifts assist the gift of prophecy. As a matter of fact, there are some gifts that the Lord uses. These gifts affect the spiritual and natural realms. Being aware of them is important. They can all be attained.

Chapter 3

Dreams

When God speaks to us in dreams, it is vital to see and interpret what God has shown us accurately. It upsets me when I hear preachers speaking against God speaking in dreams. There was one particular pastor in Nashville, TN, who would convince his members not to listen to dreams they'd have. If I had followed those directions, my ministry would not have reached the point to where it currently is. God said He'd speak in a dream or vision if there is a prophet (Numbers 12:6). God is speaking in dreams (Job 33:14-15).

Our faith manages our experiences. If we cut our faith off certain beliefs, then the opportunity for us to experience it is limited. This is why many people who don't believe in prophecy don't operate in it.

God may sometimes be direct and show us a clear vision in a dream, but there are times when symbols are used. Whether you see something directly or indirectly, like flying elephants, I believe in my deepest heart that there is something God is trying to tell you. God speaks in dreams, so we must find out and interpret what He is saying.

When I began to study dreams in the Bible, it was amazing how the Jews seemed to have a natural ability to interpret dreams effortlessly. When God started to show Joseph dreams in Genesis, he saw sheaves, stars, and other planetary bodies (moon). He saw his bundle of wheat (sheaf) rise above his brothers. His brothers immediately interpreted the dream saying, "Shalt thou reign over us?" They didn't have to go to a dream book or map the dream out. They knew how to interpret it (Genesis 37:7-8). Then he had a dream that the sun, moon, and eleven stars made obeisance to him. His father immediately interpreted it and said shalt thou father, mother, and brothers bow down to you (Genesis 37:9-10)? Other nations could not interpret the dreams they had properly. The reason was that they weren't connected to God. So, in order for them to interpret the dreams that were given, they had to get men and women of God who understood it.

God even likes to reveal things to those who are not connected to Him. Some Christians tend to believe no one speaks to anyone else but them. God tends to speak and reveal His plans to leaders. The Pharaoh of Egypt and King Nebuchadnezzar of Babylon had no communion with God at all. Yet, God said He set up Egypt and Babylon. He revealed one of the most disastrous famines of all time to Pharaoh and showed King Nebuchadnezzar the future kingdoms that would follow him. King Nebuchadnezzar even knew what the Son of God looked like before Jesus came in the flesh. God will reveal to whomever whatever He desires. In order to understand a dream or vision that is given, someone connected to the dream giver must reveal the truth, and the dream giver is Jesus.

Throughout my ministry, I have seen individuals who were far from God because of their lifestyles, receive prophetic dreams. Unfortunately, they were not able to apply what they saw to their daily lives and went around in circles. We have to remember Satan sees God on a regular basis (Job 1:6), but he is ignorant of the ultimate plan that God has for us. Some people are influenced and even possessed by demons. They may see things, but they are not aware of the plan of God.

There is someone reading this book who is a visionary. You see things others don't see. You may even hear or smell things that others don't. In order to get an applicable understanding, you have to seek the face of God. This means you need to put away fleshly desires. Even after we've put sin away, we have to remove worldly things from ourselves in a different way than others.

How do you interpret dreams?

You must interpret dreams with Jesus. The word of God is very useful for understanding dreams. It is usually best if you write the dream down. God speaks in dreams. If you see the dream and write it down as an outline, it may assist you.

The first thing you must identify are symbols. Basic elements like water, fire, wind, and dirt are crucial. Also, animals, major landmarks, and people are keys to discovering the purpose of a dream. In the past, I've seen water in my dreams. Water usually represents either judgment or cleansing. Is the water clear? Is the water murky? I will then match them up with biblical symbols of clear or murky water. A clear water would usually represent cleansing. I would have to seek God's face to understand what He was showing me. Fire would also represent judgment or testing. Utilizing your Bible is essential when interpreting dreams.

Another thing to identify are people. The people that you see in dreams don't always mean the people that you know. It may be someone with a similar personality or spirit. There are times when I dream I am the person doing something but God is showing me someone else. He just wants me to be in their shoes. In many cases, if you dream of yourself doing something that you would never do, God is showing you someone else, but He wants you to experience them in their shoes.

People dream differently. When some individuals dream, everything in the dream is the opposite of what it is in real life. Others dream the exact thing they see in reality. Some people dream and experience previous places that they've been. Knowing what is seen and when it is seen is vital. Understanding the roles of influential people in your life is also essential. If you dream the opposite things, you must interpret them in an opposing way. If you dream identically, you must interpret identically.

In some dreams, God can be testing your character. God is always trying to evolve us. Without experiencing certain tests in the natural, God may present them in a dream.

You may need to see something for yourself to get an understanding. You may want God to give you a dream on a particular issue. In order to get a dream on a particular issue to receive clarity, there are several things you must do.

Sometimes, God may just give it to you. Other times, you have to go the extra mile. When Daniel, the other wise men, and magicians, faced death because King Nebuchadnezzar wanted his dream interpreted, Daniel had to go the extra mile to see the dream (Daniel 2:19). He first sought the mercy of God with those who were with him. When something is going on that may affect you and others you know, it's best if you have them to seek God on a subject with you. God places us in connection with others at certain times. He stopped all other activities and focused on this matter. God gave him a night vision of what he needed to see. We must reason with God and ask Him for mercy.

Another thing to do, in order to get a dream or a vision, is fasting. After Daniel fasted, he had a Christophany (Daniel 10). When we fast, we push fleshly things aside and go on a spiritual walk. Every time I usually fast, I begin to have more dreams and visions. When you wake up, be ready to write it down and dissect it.

God speaks through dreams. Even if our dream seems ridiculous and crazy, if you write it down and seek God, He will give you the meaning of it, and the meaning may blow your mind. Symbols in dreams to look for are plants, animals, locations, people (types of people), time periods in life, what was done, colors, light, darkness, sin, good deeds, and most of all, Jesus. Putting these things together could answer questions and point to what God is trying to tell you.

Plants and animals are very symbolic in dreams. Wild dogs, for instance, usually represent demons. Types of plants could represent strength. Some plants with good aromas could describe a person's righteous lifestyle. Certain trees can represent prosperity (Zechariah 1:8). Certain trees can represent judgment (Jeremiah 1:11).

Colors are also very powerful. Remember always to use the word of God. For instance, royal colors could represent God's presence or riches. Red and white represent cleansing. You must use the word of the Lord to understand the colors you see and how they are applied to what you see. You will have a better understanding and a better direction in life if you interpret these dreams correctly. Others will come to you and understand their dreams. You will be able to minister Jesus to them from what they saw. We will talk more about dreams in volume 2.

Most people desire to have the spiritual gifts for the sake of just having the gifts. To have a dynamic move of

God affect you and those who follow you, you must do the extraordinary. Some things get God's attention on us. Some people may not have to do what I am about to instruct you in order to display extraordinary spiritual gifts. If you are going to truly change someone's life through spiritual gifts, you need to be smeared with the presence of Jesus. If you have an encounter with Jesus, you will never be the same nor will others who are around you.

Chapter 4

The Spirit Realm

As mentioned before, spiritual gifts are for the spirit realm, and they affect natural things. Spirits run all things. God is a Spirit. Paul said to the Ephesian church, "For we wrestle not against flesh and blood, but against principalities, against powers, against the rulers of the darkness of this world, against spiritual wickedness in high places" (Ephesians 6:12). In other words, the things that flesh and blood do is not from flesh and blood. They are either motivated by the Holy Spirit, or evil spirits drive them. The things that people do is not because of people. Spirits control people. We battle against principalities which are princes over provinces. There are governmental authorities that are not all in righteous standings. If you think about it, what happens if a demon possessed person gets into a political office? This is what Paul was talking about. There were people with evil spirits in high places, even the church. I even look at the state that many churches are falling into. Some churches are supporting gay marriage, premarital sex, abortions, and even witchcraft. I've heard ministers recommend using sorcery to members. The devil has a motive, and he has demons in place in many high positions.

We are to utilize our spiritual gifts to attack the spirit realm. Every person is ran by a spirit. The Holy Spirit motivates some, but not everyone. There are no void people. If the Holy Spirit isn't there, an evil spirit is there. It may not be active at all times, but they present themselves from time to time. Evil spirits can use even people with the Holy Spirit. Jesus walked with the disciples, and still, two of them got possessed by the devil himself (Matthew 16:23, Luke 22:3).

Peter was Jesus' right-hand man. Some people refer to him as the underdog of the ministry, and Satan temporarily possessed him (Matthew 16:23). Jesus began to prophesy about how he was to die and be raised from the dead; Peter rebuked him for saying that and Jesus immediately realized that Satan had possessed him. Jesus said to him, "Get thee behind me, Satan." He knew who he was addressing, and he handled him. Too many times, believers underestimate who they are dealing with. If you deal with people blindly, they can try to thwart the move of God and hinder prophecy.

Judas also was possessed. He ate from the very hand of Jesus and kissed Jesus' face, yet Satan was still inside of him. As he was at the table having the last supper, Jesus fed him out of his hand and then Satan entered (John 13:27). This proves that we can be close to the Lord and an evil spirit can still enter us. This is why we must be strong in the Lord. Spirits use weak-willed people. Spirits also tend to use some of those who have been close to Jesus. This is how so many pastors and spiritual leaders have been caught up in different scandals. Just because you have experienced Jesus doesn't mean that you are exempt from error. In order to cast out devils, you can't just experience Jesus. You have to be strong!

Spiritual possession is often common. Many people are operating under spiritual influences, and they are utterly blind to it. There are hints to show whether a spirit is inside a person and what spirit it is. The first thing is the appearance of a person. We are taught not to judge a person by appearance, but seeing their appearance is key. Spirits tend to mimic one another. REMEMBER, ALL SIN HAS A SPIRITUAL CONNECTION (Genesis 4:5-9). Spirits have rule over sin. When you sin, you are partnering with the spirit, and you serve the spirit that rules that sin (John 8:34; Romans 6:20). You must use the discernment of spirits.

Spirits change the appearance of a person. Let's look at some sins that are done on a global scale. Prostitution is something that has been around for millenniums. To this date, no formal education must be done for it. Yet, a prostitute in Asia dresses and presents herself almost the same as a prostitute in America. Homosexuality is something else that has been around for millenniums. A homosexual in Canada presents him or herself in the same way as one does in Africa. This is not a coincidence. Even men and women who are not open about their sexuality present tendencies that they cannot control. The reason for this is because of the spirit that controls that sin. Spirits consider the human body to be their home (Matthew 12:44). Jesus mentioned this as He spoke of spiritual possession. Anyone who owns a house decorates it. Spirits adorn people to resemble themselves.

When anyone has a home, they change it to reflect themselves. They paint it, put curtains up, some people even go to the extent of moving it depending on how the home is made. When spirits enter into a body, they change the appearance. Look at groups of people who live sinful lifestyles. Don't look to judge, look to discern. Who is there?

Spirits affect and can change the locations, scents, certain facial features, voices, walks, and most of the behavior of individuals. Individuals who operate in sin tend to congregate in particular areas, and they are attracted to one another. People who have drinking issues hang around others with a drinking problem. People who use drugs hang around others that abuse it. Spirits also try to impart themselves to others by influencing them to do likewise. There are certain spirits over sins that look for people who've been previously affected by that spirit in order to use them again. Spirits use bodies.

Some people with certain gifts of discernment can smell spirits. There was a young lady that used to attend our meetings. During this time, Jesus was upgrading my gift of discernment. I smelled a scent on her that was strange. Everyone used to compliment her on how great she smelled and how joyous she was, but this one day, while she stood next to me, something on her smelled unpleasant. God told me that it was the spirit of depression. Others without the gift of discernment couldn't smell it, but it reeked in my nostrils. The next day, she called me to tell me she was contemplating suicide. I detected the spirit, but I didn't attack it when I noticed it. Spirits give odors. If you have the gift of discernment, you may have experienced smelling odors of spirits. If so, connect smells to memory so that when you smell it again, you can remember who you are dealing with.

When you have detected a spirit, it is important to address it and attack it. Because I only detected the spirit and didn't address it, it almost took her and completed its mission. Every spirit has the mission to kill, steal, and destroy. Its goal is to kill the body, steal the inheritance, and destroy it all. Too many people entertain spirits. We are not meant to entertain them. This is why many people are defeated in churches. No one is addressing the spirits that make themselves manifested. If you know someone is operating in a particular issue or sin, you address it and that spirit. If you detect anyone with a spirit that has attached itself to them, attack it. We will discuss how to attack spirits more in the last chapter.

SPIRITS AND PEOPLE

There are many reasons spirits attach themselves to people. One of the reasons is sin. A person who operates in a particular sin and the spirit that is associated with it attaches itself to them. Also, someone who is operating in sin, their spouse or children can be affected by spirits that are associated with them.

There was a man that went to our meetings who was married. He was struggling with sexual sins, and whenever he would fall, his wife would get sick for no reason. After we prayed with them, the Lord uncovered this. Several spirits were entering his home whenever he fell. God gave us instructions for him to go home and bless his house. He said as he blessed his home, he saw several spirits leave his home and go out of the door. He went and prayed for his wife, and the Lord healed her.

Witchcraft is another reason spirits attach themselves to people. If an individual is not entirely covered in Jesus, they can be susceptible to spiritual attacks. If a person entertains witchcraft, psychics, and fortune telling, there are spirits assigned to them. Generational curses also cause spirits to attach themselves. A spirit's goal is to destroy an entire family.

There was another young lady that was in our ministry whose mother died when she was 12, in a car crash by a drunk driver. The young lady was driving one day, and she heard a demon tell her that he was going to kill her the same way he killed her mother. The young lady was in her early 20s. At this time, eight cars she owned had been totaled from accidents, and only one was her fault. These things are not coincidences. The spirit world is serious, and as a prophet, you should know how to deal with it appropriately. Shortly after, she was in a head-on collision on the highway with a drunk driver.

Praise Jesus, she was saved and didn't die. She walked out of the accident with only one scratch. Jesus will protect you. The emergency team that came out saw her car scattered all over the highway. The team leader thought for sure whoever was driving that car was dead. But God intervened.

SPIRITS AND SICKNESS

Spirits can cause illnesses, deformities, and other physical issues. Many sicknesses have medical excuses, but I am thoroughly convinced that every illness comes from a spirit and some even come from God as a form of judgment or to get their attention. Since the Lord has blessed me with the gift of healing, all of the healings that have taken place, that I've witnessed, had spiritual ties. So far, I've seen God heal cancer, kidney failure, back pain, headaches, paralysis, crippled, allergies, and high blood pressure. Every single one of these had been caused by spirits. When God is about to heal, the first thing I have to do is find the source of the sickness. After discovering the source, it must be dealt with. There are many sicknesses that doctors can't explain. Every single one of them can be traced in the spirit realm. There are multiple reasons for sickness and spirits are one of the leading causes.

SPIRITS AND PROPERTY

Spirits like property. Some properties are haunted for a reason. Spirits don't just desire the person's body; they want their real estate. There was a home behind my childhood home and every family that moved in would suffer from gun violence. It was four different families that lived in the house since I moved there and someone in each family would get shot. A spirit was in control of that home. There was only one family that didn't suffer from that. That family attended our church, and I believe that God protected them from that spirit that was over that home. They eventually moved out, and the next family that moved in, someone got shot. Spirits want to take over properties so that they can have more families to destroy.

They can also take over regions and countries. In Ezekiel 28, the king of Tyre was possessed by Satan himself. So Satan ruled that region. Before Jesus came to rescue us, every leader in the world was either possessed by a demon or was an inbred demon. Even the sanctuaries had priests that were possessed by devils (Matthew 4 and John 8:44). Satan approached Jesus and offered him all the kingdoms of the world. He couldn't do anything like that unless he owned it. And he owned it. This is why there were so many barbaric activities during those times because Satan and his cohorts were the ones controlling and influencing men. The way to prove this is through studying history.

After Jesus died, the world powers were switched. No longer did nations who were polytheistic have rule, but Christian countries were then the world powers.

Let's think about it. Rome was the world power at that time. Their civilization worshipped many gods. After Jesus died and rose again, their empire fell along with their gods. We will discuss this in Understanding and Maximizing the Gifts of Prophecy Volume 2.

When there was the original war in heaven between God and his angels and Satan and his angels 1/3 of them fell to the earth. The number of angels that fell was in the billions. Why would the Hindu culture conjure up 32 million gods and idols? Where did dragons develop from in the Asian culture? How would someone create witchcraft? An intellectual could not just come up with this type of thing. These countries with demons ruled the world, and Satan's statement to Jesus made that evident. But Jesus gave us the power to overcome the devil and his kingdom. The most that we have to do to conquer them is fast, but on an easy day, we trample over them (Luke 10:19). That is why these countries with multiple gods are no longer world powers. Christian nations are world powers now.

Spirits can possess individuals. Most of the time, we think of a demon-possessed person as being someone crawling on the ground and acting monstrously. This happens also, but there are times when demons will be inside of a person and act seemly normal.

Demons like positions of power. The same way Satan influenced the prince of Tyre, he also sways leaders. Judas sat at the table with Jesus, walked with Him, and even ate out of His hand, and Satan later possessed him. Satan temporarily possessed Peter, and Jesus identified it. He uses people of influence to get his agenda accomplished (Matthew 16:23). Paul even recognized that there were demons in high positions (Ephesians 6:12). They want power. You'd be surprised at some popular individuals who are possessed.

It's very easy to identify those who are possessed. Anyone who can carry out Satan's agenda and message is possessed. It may be temporary or permanent. Whether it's temporarily or continually, they are. Anyone who convinces others to sin is being managed by that spirit. Our job as a believer and prophet first, is to identify it and then defeat it.

Chapter 5

Basic Abilities of Prophets

Prophets can do amazing things. Paul referred to the gift of prophecy as being the best gift. We will only discuss 17 main abilities of prophets. There are more, but these are merely the basics. Why is there more? Because God is not limited. He is limitless which means He cannot be limited to what I am listing.

The first thing that we will discuss is the ability to see the past. With the gift of the word of knowledge, this allows individuals to know stuff from the past that a stranger should not be aware. Daniel saw a previous dream that King Nebuchadnezzar had (Daniel 2). Nathan the prophet knew that David slept with Bathsheba and had her husband to be placed on the front line of battle to be killed (2 Samuel 12). As we operate in our gifts and communicate with God, He will reveal hidden things to us.

The next thing we will discuss are current events. As prophets, God will reveal current events for us to effectively minister and encourage those we are called to. Samuel the prophet saw that King Saul did wrong from the Lord (1 Samuel 15). Peter saw that Ananias and Sapphire told a lie (Acts 5). The Lord even revealed their business dealing to him.

God is an accurate God, and He has goals for us to accomplish. Elisha the prophet knew the secret deed that his servant did. His servant went behind his back to get the wealth that Naaman the leper brought (2 Kings 5). He will reveal secrets to prophets in order to get His work accomplished and even to keep His prophets informed.

The Lord also allows prophets to see the future. The Lord was reminding Abraham of the promise in Genesis 18, but while He was there, He pondered whether He should reveal to Abraham what would become of Sodom and Gomorrah. God said that because Abraham was about to be great, He would reveal it to him. Abraham learned of what would happen to those cities before it happened and he interceded for them. He also revealed to Abraham that his descendants would be slaves in Egypt. This happened hundreds of years later (Genesis 17 and 18). Moses was informed of how Pharaoh would respond every time he would approach him (Exodus 7:3). Jeremiah and Isaiah saw a lot of future events. Isaiah knew that King Hezekiah was going to die soon. Isaiah also knew what Jesus looked like before He even came (Isaiah 53). A true prophet is known when his word comes to pass.

Another thing that prophets can do is interpret spiritual encounters. Joseph was present to interpret the pharaoh's dream. Daniel was present to decipher the writing on the wall. Remember that spirits can affect reality. When there are realistic encounters, a prophet is needed to explain what is being stated.

Prophets can control the weather and cause natural disasters. Elijah prophesied a drought that killed many people. He didn't just prophesy it, but he caused it. The Lord told him to speak it (1 Kings 17). It had to be spoken for it to occur. God can cause anything to happen, but there will be times when He gives the ability to do a natural phenomenon to occur by the hand or mouth of a prophet. The same prophet spoke for the rain to return (1 Kings 18). He even prayed fire from heaven to come and consume an altar. Joshua was able to control the orbit of the earth. In order to have victory in battle, Joshua stopped natural time, and the sun did not set (Joshua 10). Jesus was amazed at His disciples when they came to Him because of a storm while they were at sea. He spoke calmness to the storm. Even Moses caused natural phenomenon to happen. Water turned into blood by his hand. Fiery hail rained from the sky on Egypt as well. We have the ability to control the weather.

I must personally interject on this subject. As I studied this years ago, I decided to put my belief into action. I would regularly go jogging. One day, while I was jogging, it began to rain. I almost turned around and went home, but I thought about what I had just been studying. So, instead, I stopped and gave the earth attention to who I was in God. I then commanded the rain to stop. It stopped. I thought to myself; maybe this is a coincidence. So, I demanded it to begin to rain again. Seconds later, it started to rain. I knew what God could do, but for a moment, I thought to myself, I must be crazy. So, I continued jogging in the rain. I stopped again and told the earth who I was again and commanded that the rain stopped. The rain stopped. I kept this in my heart.

Time went on, and I began to hold a series of outdoor events. We were about to have a huge one, and there were terrible storms in the area. It was storming the whole day. I had my faith and confidence that I could control the weather with Jesus. People began to message me to ask if we should cancel it. I said no, it would not be raining in our area. They warned me that all of the forecasts announced that it would continue to rain that day and all through next week. I said it would stop. I stood up and did the same thing that I did when I was jogging. I told the earth who I was in relation to Jesus and commanded that it didn't rain in our area. The entire time of our event, the sun was shining, and the ground dried up. The weird part about it was that it rained everywhere around our event as if a circle was made around the place. People came in amazement that it was not raining there. I laughingly told them that I could control the weather in Jesus. As soon as the event ended, the storm returned in its wrath. The same thing happened for the next three events. As a matter of fact, I lived a mile away, and my wife said that it was storming so bad that the lights went out. The whole time where I was, the sun was shining. I have done the same thing when traveling, and bad weather would come. If I am on a spiritual mission, I tell the weather what I need it to do.

Another thing that prophets can do is transcend communication barriers. This is with all things. We have the ability to speak to nature. We can even communicate with animals. Balaam spoke with his ass (Numbers 22). Elisha caused a bear to devour children who mocked him (2 Kings 2). Moses had flies, lice, and frogs to plague the land of Egypt. Jesus spoke to the storm. The Lord uses all things, so in the line of communication with the prophet, all nature is open for interaction.

Prophets can control royalty. The only way to fully control royalty in the natural world is to form alliances or overtake the royal kingdom with war. A prophet has the power to rule over royalty. They don't need to cause war or make alliances to get to the kingdom. Pharaoh referred to Joseph as father in Genesis. Even though Joseph was second in command, the Pharaoh answered to him. Moses had to deal with a Pharaoh as well. John spoke with Herod. Prophets deal with leaders.

When the enemy comes in like a flood, the Lord raises up a standard (Isaiah 59:19). In many cases, the prophet was considered the standard. Egyptians were bearing hard on the Israelites, and the Lord raised up Moses as the standard. Ahab allowed evil to reign, and the Lord raised up Elijah. The entire Book of Judges shows how evil would rise and then God would raise up a judge with the gift of prophecy. All throughout the Holy Scriptures, the Lord would raise up prophets during times of turmoil.

Prophets also can change the fates of people and even nations. Prophets are close to God. Moses was close. The children of Israel knew God's acts, but Moses knew His ways (Psalms 103:7). God was about to wipe the children of Israel out of existence. Moses interceded for them, and God spared those who were on His side. If it weren't for Moses jumping in, they would've all been killed. Isaiah gave the word to Hezekiah that he should get his house in order because he was about to die. If he had not given that word, Hezekiah would've been unaware of his fate, and he wouldn't have been able to have God to change that prophetic word around. Hezekiah had 15 years added on to his life because of the warning and his response. As prophets, we can change the fates of individuals if we speak to God and speak to the people.

Prophets have the ability to curse. Noah cursed Canaan from simply speaking a word. When someone did Abraham wrong, curses were sent (Genesis 12:17). Abram said that Sarai was his sister and deceived Pharaoh. Because of this, God sent a curse to his house. Elisha cursed children that mocked him and caused bears to come and devour them (2 Kings 2:24).

Prophets have the power to bless. Prophets can leave peace over a home. Jesus said if a home is worthy and they receive you, then leave your peace (Matthew 10:13). I have done this on multiple occasions. I would sometimes purposefully lodge with someone to leave a blessing. There was a man who was unemployed, and I had to go to his city to minister. I lodged there at his home. I left my peace there. He had been unemployed for over a year. When I left, God instructed me to tell him that the first week of March, he would get the job he wanted. He got three job offers in the month of March, and the position he chose paid him four times more than he made on his previous job. I left my peace there.

We speak to God. How will they hear without a preacher? God speaks to His prophets. We receive the messages, and for those who are not listening to God or if they have something stopping them from hearing Him, we are there to relay the message.

We can make referrals as well to bless others. If you receive a prophet in the name of a prophet, you will receive a prophet's reward (Matthew 10:41). This means if you want to bless someone, you can refer them to a prophet and they will receive that prophet's reward or blessing. Referring people to prophets as a prophet blesses them.

I did this for a friend of mine who was unemployed for a long period of time. The jobs he did have were low-paying. I referred him to a female prophet I knew in New Orleans. I told him to send her a $10 seed. When he sent it, the next day, God blessed him with a job paying $55,000 a year with benefits. Now, he and his wife own a business, and he is making over $100,000 a year from his business. He quit his job and now pursues music. As a prophet, you can refer others to other real prophets and bless them.

We have dominance over spirits. Believers should have this ability as well. But if they do not, we can cast out spirits (Matthew 10). Spirits are the primary cause for most of the turmoil in the world. That is why the spiritual gift of prophecy is needed.

The last thing I will mention in this section is that we have the ability to heal the sick and raise the dead. Elisha prophesied the Shunammite's woman son into life. The boy died, and the prophet was called back to raise him up. Jesus gave a commandment for His disciples to heal the sick and raise the dead in Matthews 10. We have the power to heal. We have the power of life and death in our tongue when it's given from God.

Chapter 6

God's use of spirits

As prophets, I believe that it is crucial to understand the spirit realm. In my ministry, the Lord has healed and delivered many because of Him allowing me to understand the spirit realm. The same way He has allowed me to understand it and deliver others who have been oppressed by demons, in like manner I want you to be able to set others free.

God uses spirits to accomplish His goals. Most Christians look at God and His works through the eyes of sweetness, but God spoke with Isaiah, and He said, "I make peace, and create evil: I the Lord do all these things" (Isaiah 45:7). He also told Moses that He makes the "dumb, deaf, seeing, and the blind" (Exodus 4:11). God referred to Esau as the one He hated (Romans 9:13). The Lord revealed to me that He still uses spirits to get His work accomplished.

There are spirits of darkness and spirits of light. For those who use the path of darkness, spirits of darkness are sent to cause their demise. Those who are on God's path, He uses His spirits. There are times when spirits of darkness are used on people who walk in God's light as well.

God uses spirits to send judgment. Ahab was unrighteous, and his wife corrupted the house of God. She murdered prophets and had Jews worshipping Baal. Ahab was supposed to be on the Lord's side completely. So, God decided to send a spirit to him. In 2 Chronicles 18:19-21, God held a presentation to a group of spirits. A spirit came forth and said he would be a lying spirit in the mouth of the prophets to cause the fall of Ahab. A godly man named Jehoshaphat got in the crossfire of spiritual activity and almost died because of his connection to Ahab (2 Chronicles 18:31). God used that spirit to achieve His agenda.

Jehoshaphat was a godly leader, but because of his ties with Ahab, he experienced a spiritual attack. He was surrounded by warriors to kill him, but He cried out to God, and God caused them to leave. That spirit was supposed to orchestrate Ahab to be in that spot, but because of Jehoshaphat, the two of them got mixed. That lying spirit's agenda almost killed a man of God. This is how believers, who are living righteously, undergo attacks sometimes. They may be connected with the wrong people or be in the wrong place. Our job is to get them to cry to God and be repositioned.

God uses spirits to reposition believers. David was playing the harp for Saul. Saul began to prophesy, and the Lord sent a murdering spirit on Saul, and he took a javelin and threw it at David. This happened twice (1 Sam 18:10 and 1 Sam 19:9-11). David was walking in purity. I wondered why God would send a murderous spirit against David? David was already anointed as king, but he hadn't walked into his position yet to fulfill the prophecy. Why would God do this? The Lord shared with me that he had to reposition David. He caused this to happen for David to flee and become stronger than what he was. He had to cultivate survival skills, and he ended up returning with his own army. He was able to convert men who were considered no good and turned them into men of valor (1 Chronicles 12:21). If it weren't for God sending that spirit on Saul to attack David, he possibly would have stayed and never acquired his skills and resources. God used that spirit to accomplish His agenda.

There are times when God will allow someone to be possessed with a spirit to get us to move and get somewhere else. If David wouldn't have been attacked by that spirit, that the Lord sent to possess Saul, he may not have reached the growth that he needed to reach. He will allow spirits to move on people around you to reposition you. Where I am now is because of attacks by others who had evil spirits, and it allowed me to get more resources and become a stronger man in Christ. Like a great father, God wants us to grow and mature.

For those of us who fully belong to God, we can't be controlled by Satan. Be aware. If any portion of your heart belongs to the enemy, to the point where we serve sin, the enemy can easily infiltrate our bodies. Whoever sins is a servant to sin (John 8:34). There is no way to be a servant to something that has no life. We cannot serve objects. Even inanimate objects are connected to the people that control them. The same thing applies to sin. Sin has spirit connections and whoever sins serves the spirit that is the master of that sin.

When we fully belong to God, He will not control us. He guides our path. Believe it or not, those who do not belong to God are fully controlled by Him. An example of this is found in Exodus 7:13 when the Lord hardened pharaoh's heart to prevent him from freeing the children of Israel. The Lord made him do that, but He did not force the children of Israel to serve Him. Those of us who belong to God have softer hearts, which are for God, but we have our own will. The Lord had Caesar to make a decision to send people back to their cities to be taxed (Luke 2:1-7). This was a move of God to get Jesus to Bethlehem to fulfill prophecy. The Lord controlled Nebuchadnezzar to conquer Jerusalem

(Jeremiah 6:22). For the believer, He leaves instructions for us to follow and He will guide us using everything He created, but the ungodly are controlled.

God uses everything that He created. God controls even demons. Satan does not have that much authority to where he has his own freedom. Too many Christians give Satan too much credit, but in order to do anything or affect even the believer, He has to get permission from God. Remember, God even uses demons. A lot of times, we think that Satan is randomly looking to attack us, but there are times when God will present you to Satan for an attack. Yes, Satan does go about like a roaring lion seeking whom he may devour (1 Peter 5:8), but there are times when he is on an assignment by God. Let's go to the Word of God to prove this.

Satan didn't come to God to make a presentation to Him about Job. As a matter of fact, the sons of God came to Him, and Satan was among them, but it was God that mentioned Job to Satan. God asked Satan, have you considered my servant Job? God brought Job up to Satan, and they created the dialog from there on what would happen to his family and life. Even in the story of 2 Chronicles 18:21, God sought a spirit to entice Ahab. The spirits didn't bring it up to God; God brought it up to them. In 1 Samuel 18:10, God sent an evil spirit on Saul to attempt to kill David. As a matter of fact, there were multiple occasions where God sent evil spirits on people. There will be times when God brings our names up even to Satan, but He has a purpose in it all. God wanted Job to go deeper and receive a revelation from Him (Job 38). God wanted to drive David off from Israel (1 Samuel 19:10). God wanted to judge Ahab (2 Chronicles 18:21). In all three scenarios, God used a spirit to do something to the believer. He may use spirits to get us to a place of better understanding, even if it means turning our world upside down. He may use spirits to attack us so we can be repositioned as well.

An example in my life of this was in 2013 when I was an insurance adjuster. During this time, I was not able to do any ministry endeavors because I worked 84 hours a week on this job. My wife and I just discovered we were expecting a baby. We were making great money, so we had no concerns. Two weeks after finding out we were expecting a baby, I went on a fast. At the end of my fast, I saw a demon at my job in the middle of the building. Whenever I see spirits, I rebuke them and cast them away to be tortured because we have that ability in Christ. No demons should dwell where we are. Shortly after I saw the demon, I was fired unjustly because someone lied on me. For months, I could not find a job. I wondered why this happened. I went on another fast, and at the end of the fast, God blessed me with my own business. From that point on, neither my wife nor I had to work, and I had plenty of time to spend with my family. I then realized that the Lord sent that demon there to get me fired. I gave God thanks for allowing me to get fired because if I hadn't gotten fired, I would have never started my own company. So, no matter what happens, I know there is a purpose in what happens in my life. Even if it seems bad, God is in complete control.

God allowed that spirit to disrupt me so that I could get my own resources. My purpose was not with that job. I was there for a season, but God wanted me to begin my own company. That spirit was sent on an assignment.

As a sold-out believer in Christ, you must understand that we are not going through a series of random events. God has everything in order. If a believer is being affected by a demon, it is for a reason. I will talk about the two of them.

The first reason God would send a spirit to affect a believer is because He has sent judgment. Saul was tormented by a demon which was sent from the Lord (1 Samuel 16:14). Saul was disobedient. This was the second occasion where he did not follow directions. Because he didn't follow directions, the Lord took His Spirit from him and replaced it with an evil spirit. There are times when believers are disobedient, and judgment comes. He chastises His children.

Saul was a believer in God, he was anointed, and he had the gift of prophecy. He didn't obey God, and he was prideful. Because of this, the Lord rejected him and took away his anointing.

When we disobey, we step out of the protection and peace of Jesus. Many believers in Christ no longer believe we must obey Him. Many claim to love God, but because of disobedience, they have been in judgment. There are times I go to visit or minister at other churches, and I see believers surrounded by defeat. The reason for this is because of disobedience. Samuel said that it's better to obey than sacrifice. When we are disobedient, there is an availability for a spirit to torment us.

Demons would regularly come to Saul to bother him. As a reminder, the scripture said that in both cases, the spirit was sent from the Lord (1 Samuel 18:10 and 1 Samuel 19:9-11). God has control over good and evil spirits. This means that there is nothing that can catch us unaware. We belong to Jesus.

The second reason God would send a spirit is to reposition us. As we mentioned earlier, a demon came on Saul on two different occasions. This time, the demon didn't do anything to hurt Saul. As a matter of fact, when the spirit came on him, he began to prophesy. While he was prophesying with a demon in him, he tried to kill David with a javelin. We are reminded again that the evil spirit came from God. This spirit caused Saul to attempt murder, but to someone who was now carrying the anointing of God. When I read that, I thought to myself, why would God send an evil spirit on Saul to try and kill David? The Lord later shared with me that He was repositioning David and He used that evil spirit to do it.

When we are walking upright and in our purpose for Christ, and we undergo attacks, we must be aware that God runs all things. So, if there is something that seems like it is disturbing you or it is some type of spiritual attack, we must be aware of why this is happening because God is trying to do something with us. God needed David to leave Israel before he would return to become king. God will control others just to get them to position us. God didn't make the Israelites do anything. He made Pharaoh do things. He hardened his heart so that he could do what He wanted to do. He can control the emotions of the unbeliever, and their decisions will be based on something they were forced to do. It is the opposite for a believer. Many believers just want to be like robots and have God make us do things, but God orders our footsteps. He will not force us to do anything. He will control nature, ungodly men and women, and even animals to position us where we should be in His ultimate plan for our promise.

Jonah was a great example of someone who God ordered. He told Jonah to go to Nineveh. He didn't force him by controlling his decisions. First, God changed the weather which caused the ship Jonah was on to be troubled, thus leading him to being thrown overboard. Next, he used a whale (animal) to swallow him up just so he could fast, repent, and go to Nineveh. God will alter the very course of nature to guide our footsteps appropriately. He would allow things to go wrong to get us on the right path.

All of this is to say that God will use anything and everything to get us on the path he has for us. Demons are not exempt from that. As we read in scriptures earlier, He used demons on Saul and Ahab. As long as we stay on a path of righteousness with God, demons can't control us internally. Yet, even though we follow Jesus, we can still possibly be possessed by a demon. We must be sure to be strong in Christ to resist the enemy.

Chapter 7

The Power of Prophets against Spirits

As prophets, we have the power over demons. When we encounter a demon, we must first identify him and then attack. Many sicknesses are in demonic realms. When people open themselves up to spirits, they enter in and begin to cause death. As prophets, we must identify the origin of illness so that we can be able to decipher and discern what needs to be done to remedy it. Seeing it is just the first step.

Unfortunately, many demons have crept into the church. This is not a new issue. This was occurring even before Jesus came. Many denominations are still carrying on the work of the church but many demons have crept in, and the saints are affected by it. When prophets are under demonic influence, it is very evident. Many of the elect in Christ are still deceived, but when you have your eyes opened, you can clearly see. Jesus even said that there are false prophets that will try to deceive the ones who belong to God (Matthew 24:24).

Let's revisit a scripture we discussed in 2 Chronicles 18:21. A spirit came forth in the presence of God and said that he would be a lying spirit in the mouth of the prophets and God allowed him to be so. Even the prophet Micaiah wasn't exempt from this lying spirit. He saw the same things that the other prophets saw. But before he saw what they saw, he saw the truth. The other prophets had been infiltrated with Baal worship and idolatry due to Jezebel. As true prophets, we must be mindful of our affiliations with others because it can verily taint the very message that we preach. Micaiah ended up revealing what truly happened because he had a connection to God. If we have a connection to God, we will see what is going on.

The same thing that happened to Micaiah happened to me once. One of my colleagues in Christ decided to run for mayor. I had a dream, a week before she informed me that she was going to run, that she got in third place, which really held no placement, but in the dream, she was still in that position for mayor despite being in the third place. She called me a week after I had the dream to inform me she was running for that political seat that I saw in my dream. Other men and women of God were telling her that she would win and to take the seat. When I shared my dream, she believed the interpretation was that there would be three people total running for that position, which was true. I simply went along with that. From that point on, the dreams that I had was that she was going to win. At the end of the race, she lost and got third place as my original dream was. I was pulled in by other prophets who were affected by the lying spirit. I believe God wanted her to run for that position. There is no doubt in my mind about that. But I saw the correct thing in the beginning. After I got involved, I saw what the other prophets saw. False prophets were still affecting believers after Jesus. Paul had to regularly warn his believers of ravening wolves which were false prophets (Romans 16:17-27).

As prophets, we must be aware of demons and cast them out. Demons try to hide. Many people have become oblivious to demonic activity. Many believers assume that because someone goes to church, quotes scriptures, and says God that they are clear of spirits. This is true even outside of the church. People think this about people who do evil as well. When they hear them say Jesus we put our safety guards down and follow them. Demons, Christians, and prophets have several things in common. In the Book of Luke 8 and Mark 5, the demon Legion entered into a man. The demons did several things that Christians and prophets were able to do. These are common grounds that demons and Christians have:

1. Worship: He worshipped Jesus (Mark 5:6). This is something I was taught was exclusive to believers. This was wrong. Throughout the scripture, there are instances when demons and even Satan was before God's throne. David told dragons to praise God (Psalms 148:7). The demons fell at the feet of Jesus and worshipped Him (Mark 5:6). Even demons fear and tremble (James 2:19).

2. Calling Jesus' name: The demon Legion called on Jesus name (Mark 5:7). I was taught at the name of Jesus, demons must flee, but that isn't even a scripture. Several other scriptures show demons saying the very name of Jesus.

3. Prayer: He made a request to Jesus, and it was answered (Mark 5:12). They requested God to send them into the swine, and He did it.

We must be able to decipher when a demon has entered a person or place. Demons can see the past and read people. This is how witches and psychics operate. They identify similar spirits and try to predict the future. Prophets identify spirits, but God shows us the path Jesus has for their future.

So, with these three main common grounds between Christians and Demons, how can we decipher someone who is operating in the Spirit of God and someone who is possessed by a demon? Many people claim and believe that worship is something that is exclusive to the believer when the Word of God says even demons fear and tremble (James 2:19). David told dragons to praise God (Psalms 148). We see several moments in scripture where demons are presenting themselves before God's throne and finally we run into Mark chapter 5 when the demon Legion acts out the things he is able to do. Praise and worship are very important, but it isn't what differentiates us from demons. I have experienced times when a demon-possessed individual would mock the body of Christ during praise and worship.

I was living in Nashville, TN at the time and my prophetic ministry was just starting to take off. I was attending an apostolic church I would frequently visit. This day, the pastor wasn't there, and there was a praise service going on. While the praise and worship were going on, a man, who also frequently attended the church, began to act out. This man was 6 foot and 8 inches tall which was a little bit taller than me, but he was huge also. He began to pace the church. He came up and laid his cigarettes at the altar, but he didn't do it as a form of repentance. He began to march violently around the church. I immediately identified the man had a demon in him that was manifesting himself. I proceeded to go and cast the demon out of him. At this time, I had never done it, but I knew what needed to be done from my mentors and from learning from Jesus. I asked him if he wanted to pray. He said yes. When I said Jesus, he began to run. That ministry didn't teach on the spirit realm, and the ministers never experienced that. One of the ministers came to me and said to leave the man alone and let him be. While he said that, the man jumped on the pulpit and started shaking his butt in front of the congregation as the song was playing. It took four of us to pull him off the altar. We then had him cornered. That church taught heavily on spiritual tongues, so the ministers were speaking in tongues around him. The Lord told me that demon had to be cast out. At that point, I told the demon to get out of the man. When I did that, the man started vehemently coughing, and I felt the heat of a presence leave him. The spirit didn't leave the property though. Everyone thought that it was over. The man looked dazed like he had no idea what just happened. His family received a call to pick him up, so his brother came. As his brother came into the building, the demon possessed him, and he began to act out the same thing that the brother did. I went and cast the spirit out, and the demon left him and entered back into his brother. I did not know about sending demons away at that time. Finally, we got both men delivered of the demon.

That demon was able to mingle with Christians during worship and praise, but demonic praise and worship are destructive and loudly disruptive. What differentiates us from them are two key things:

1. Authority: Jesus said, "he gave us authority to tread over serpents, scorpions, and over all the power of the enemy (Luke 10:19)." In Acts 16, two men tried to cast out demons, and they attacked them because they didn't have the authority to do so.
2. Truth: Satan is the father of lies, and the truth is not in him (John 8:44). We have the truth of the Word of Jesus. God's word is His truth (John 17:17).

When we walk in our spiritual authority by not succumbing to sin, we can defeat the enemy. Our authority in Christ prevents demons from even entering us. Our authority is what is able to defeat them.

It is not just the name of Jesus that defeats demons, but it is the power we possess in that name. The demon Legion said Jesus' name, but if we have the authority of Christ and

His identity, demons will be running because of what is on the inside of us even before we open our mouth.

Growing up, I was taught that if I said the name of Jesus, demons would flee. When I began to deal with them, I quickly learned that it wasn't just saying the name that caused demons to leave. I had to have authority. If I didn't have authority, demons could attack me (Acts 19:15). There were Jews who tried to cast out a demon, and because they lacked the authority, the demon jumped on them and beat them up.

As a prophet, I had to learn how to deal with spirits. Spirits are what cause a lot of the world's issues. There are spirits everywhere, and they motivate people and even control things. Satan had control of the weather when he knocked down Job's son house. He influenced people to cause raiders to kill his servants and livestock. As prophets, we have control over those demons. The only one who overrides our voice is Jesus. There are times when He uses spirits to do His will. I've experienced demons causing people to be crippled in wheelchairs, have migraines, cause other illnesses, and even hinder finances. As a prophet, if I want to see that person delivered, I must attack those spirits.

We have power over demons. From the authority that God has given us, we can torture demons. Unfortunately, we see many believers with no authority over them. The main thing that causes us not to have authority over them is sin. Spirits rule over sins, and when we fall into sin, those spirits rule over us until they have been cast out.

Sin has become accepted as the norm to many believers. The church has become so comfortable with sin. Television desensitizes sin and makes it seem as if it is acceptable to everyone. Despite those who believe that it is acceptable, God doesn't care. I just want to be accepted by God.

Chapter 8

How to Utilize Our Gifts Against the Spirit Realm

When we have the authority in Christ over spirits, we simply tread over them. Not only can we tread over them, but they can come running to us in fear. When Jesus was afar off, demons nearby would come running in fear. Back to the story of the demon Legion, he came to Jesus asking that Jesus would refrain from torturing him. This showed that Jesus could torture demons (Luke 8:28).

After I realized this, I began to practice the ability that Jesus had. I pray for my family. Because they are their own individuals and make their own choices, I cannot have as much control over what happens. A couple of my family members get migraines. I realized that it wasn't just a series of random headaches the first time I saw a spirit lodged in their brain. One day, I proceeded to pray for one of them. I used discernment to see the spirit, and I commanded the spirit to leave. Her head got better moments later without her having to take medication. About an hour later, the spirit returned. I saw the same spirit. God brought back to my memory that I had the ability to torture and imprison demons. I then commanded the spirit to be beheaded and buried. I saw that spirits head come off and buried. Her headache left and didn't return until years later. The Lord revealed to me there were actions in her life that needed to be rectified. Until she changed her ways, the spirit would visit her periodically, but until she reactivated her actions, the spirit was imprisoned.

We have the power to cast out demons and torture them, but even after a demon has been removed, healing needs to take place. From that point on, you must put Jesus into the equation. Jesus is light, and there is healing in His light. When utilizing the ability to heal, we must find Jesus on the inside of the person needing deliverance or get Him to fill that body.

We can easily cast out devils. Yet, some devils can only come out by prayer and fasting (Matthew 17:21). We must be sensitive to the Holy Spirit. There are times when I can minister to individuals easily. When I do a prophecy conference or healing service, in order to minister to my best ability, I must fast. Fasting helps to easily separate you from the earthly platform into a spiritual platform. So, when you are dealing with individuals facing turmoil from strong spirits, God has strengthened your spirit through prayer and fasting so you can command any spirit to be tormented and imprisoned.

Things that fasting does:

Why is fasting so important? Fasting does several things.

1. Gets God attention. Our stomach and our desires are connected to God. God ensures that He feeds us. David said that he never saw the righteous forsaken nor his seed begging bread (Psalms 37:25). God has a direct link from Him to our stomachs to ensure that we are being fed. When we pull back from our desires, an alert goes off to God, and it gets His attention. This also proves to Him that we are willing to sacrifice to get what He has to offer.

2. Places our flesh in subjection. Every day, we give in to our flesh in one way or another. We may listen to our favorite song, watch our favorite show, or even do something we always enjoy. When we fast, it causes our flesh to be placed on hold and build up our spirit. King David said his flesh yearned for God (Psalms 63:1). In order to get our flesh to yearn for God, we must link the desires of our flesh with the desires of our spirit. The best way to do this is through fasting and praying.

3. Fasting makes your spirit stronger. Fasting accompanied by prayer and receiving God's Word makes our spirits stronger. This is why Jesus said that in order to cast out certain spirits, you must fast and pray. Fasting and praying get us closer to God because we aren't feeding our flesh, but rather our spirit. This curves our appetites.

I remember when I did my first fast without food for three days. I was in college. I was so hungry until I would stop, pray, and receive God's Word. After I did that, I felt like I had a full course meal. That carried me through my 3-day fast. When I returned to food, I didn't even miss it. My spirit was much stronger. I was able to combat demons. I had power over illnesses. This was because God built up my spirit.

Fasting doesn't make sense. Logically, our body needs food. The spirit world is very real. It is so real it can alter nature. As you are building your spirit through fasting, nature is getting altered in your body. When I would go on my 3-day fasts or Daniel's fasts, I would still be the same weight. The spirit realm would become so relevant that it became food to my body and sustained my weight. I've done diets where I would eat the same food as I would on a

Daniel's fast and lose weight, but I would do a Daniel's fast to seek God and I wouldn't lose any weight. God preserved and fed me spiritually on my fasts. He converted spiritual food into natural food. This is how Daniel and the three Hebrew boys were able to be finer than those who were eating the king's meat. They had access to Heaven. Heaven can alter nature (Daniel 1-2). Our mission is to tap into God's voice and get Him to move on our behalf. I will explain how to do that.

Step 1. Praise and Worship

David shared with us how to reach the voice of God. Psalms 95 says to, "Come before his presence with thanksgiving and make a joyful noise unto Him with psalms" (Psalms 95:2). Begin to remember the amazing things that the Lord has done for you throughout your life. Give Him thanks for those things that He has done and acknowledge Him for His great works. Then give Him praise for His mighty works. Boast in what God has done. He raises the dead, He has healed the sick, and He made the earth and the heavens. God inhabits the praises of His people (Psalms 22:3). When we praise God, you welcome Him to come in the midst of where you are.

Step 2. Worship

After David tells us to praise and thank God, he follows it by saying, "Let us worship and bow down: let us kneel before the Lord our maker." We then worship and adore God. We tell Him how amazingly beautiful He is. We tell Him about His holiness. We romance God. The definition of worship is, "the feeling or expression of adoration for a deity" (Webster Dictionary). Some synonyms for worship are glorification, reverence, honor, and devotion. We show passion to our Father. Telling Him how He is perfect and holy is a great way to worship Him. We worship Him in a state of humility.

Humble yourself: God accepts those with a broken spirit and a contrite heart. When we approach God (wherever you are), we come to Him humbly yet boldly. We must show an act of humbleness. Some forms of humbleness are bowing our heads or getting on our knees to acknowledge Him as God.

There have been times that I've prayed, and I do not hear His voice or feel His presence. I then I realized I never humbled myself. The moment I get on my knees, I would see Heaven open up for me. Even while I'm driving, I may bow my head briefly to show obeisance to God.

So many times, we get lazy, and we expect God to respond to us any kind of way. Jesus is our best friend, the Lover of our souls, the Son of God, our Father, and much more, but we must remember He is God. Some forms of idol worship require the subject to remain on their knees during the entire time of the ceremony. The least that we can do before we present ourselves to God is bow our heads. So, as we worship God, do it with a genuine, passionate, and pure heart. While you share your passion with God, be humble. This is the reason many people aren't prophets and can't hear God's voice. If you don't have passion for God, you cannot hold a conversation with Him to receive His secrets.

After this, God may have you to stand up and present yourself to Him as He did Ezekiel (Ezekiel 2:1). There are times when we are humble, and then there are times when we must stand.

Step 3. Listen

After we have praised God and worshiped Him according to what David said, we can then step into the prophetic. After he admonished us to praise and worship in Psalms 95:2&6,

he tells us, "Today, if you will hear His voice." He gave us the instruction on how to tap into the heavenly voice of Jesus. After we have praised God and reached the peak of worship, His voice is available. We can listen to Him. We must be still. Many people teach about being passionate with God. We must be passionate. Many people talk about making a joyful sound to God. We must be joyous with Him. Not too many people talk about silence with God. After we have reached the peak of worship, we must stop. Be sure you have your radio off, make sure you are not moving, and stop all activity in your flesh. God is before you along with His heavenly beings. David said "IF" you can hear His voice. He didn't say you will. So, how do you hear God's voice?

In order to hear God's voice, you must be still and know God (Psalm 46:10). When we are trained to be emotional at every whim, we move too much. When God shows up and begins to move, we must be still and receive what He has for us. When the Lord is raised up out of the holy place where He inhabits, we must be silent. The word of God says, "Be silent, O all flesh, before the Lord: for he is raised up out of his holy habitation" (Zechariah 2:13). There is a holy solemnness that must take place. Hearing what God has to say is so pivotal in prophecy.

Zechariah said we must be silent. When God arrives, there is nothing more important than seeing what He is about to do. He said that God is raised up out of His holy habitation. God has arrived at where you are from His holy habitation. He has moved on our behalf. So, if we are reacting from our emotions, we can entirely miss what He is about to do.

There is a time for rejoicing, and there is a period to be still. When we fellowship with one another, we give God praise and worship. Then there is a time for us to receive His word. If you have only rejoiced, but God never spoke, you didn't receive your miracle yet. We must stop all activity and be still to receive God's Word. When His Word has arrived, and we have received it completely, then it is time to rejoice.

We mix the stirring of our soul and spirit with the move of God. You can be filled in your spirit and rejoice without even being controlled by God. I've heard people said that they were shouting and dancing in church because they caught the Holy Ghost. This is not fully accurate. Our body reacts when it experiences a spiritual and even an emotional encounter. When people watch movies, and they are moved enough, they may cry. Or if a movie is scary enough, they may jump. There are times when people watch movies, and they get goosebumps. This is even more accurate when God's Spirit is involved. When we hear a word from heaven or a song that ministers to us, our spirit may get filled and we react. This does not mean you have caught the Holy Ghost. This is contrary to popular belief. When we see someone shout in church or pass out, we tend to believe they caught the Holy Ghost. We must go to God's Word to see the evidence of the Holy Ghost. Throughout the Word of God, when the Holy Ghost would fall on someone, there was something way greater than praise and worship that took place. The evidence of God's Spirit happens when the Holy Ghost comes utilizing spiritual gifts.

Ezekiel saw spiritual activity taking place with His own eyes. In chapter two, the Holy Spirit entered him, and he stood on his feet and received what the Lord had to say. This was the start of Ezekiel's ministry. He received what the Lord had to say. Many people are taught to react by passing out. There have been times when people did pass out. One other time was when a demon left out of a man in Mark 9. When John saw Jesus, he passed out as one dead but God got him up, and he received the Book of Revelation (Revelation 1:17). So, when God shows up, we must prepare to receive His word because a miracle is about to happen for us. Jesus is His word. When we receive His word, we accept Jesus. Jesus and His Word is the same thing. When we don't receive His Word, we are not accepting Jesus. That is the most important thing when dealing with prophecy. "And he hath filled him with the **spirit** of God, in wisdom" (Exodus 35:21-31).

When we receive God's Word, it is Jesus. When Jesus comes, things can change immediately. I've seen the Lord move so miraculously that even before the service would start, a miracle would take place before individuals made it to the service. When Jesus comes, we must see and know what He is doing. We can inquire of Him. Have a holy conversation with Him. He can then move.

Chapter 9

The Word

Jesus is the Word. I must go into detail on what the Word is. I believe that these last two chapters are the most important. I believe the Bible. I do not find any error in the Bible. Even though there may be controversial scriptures that are very debatable, I believe they are a mystery that must be solved. Within the Bible is the Word. The Word is Jesus. Anywhere in the Bible that says God spoke, His Word, God said, etc., it was Jesus. Even in the Old Testament. Even though we understand that Jesus was born in the New Testament, He was very present in the Old Testament as the Word. This is one of the mysteries of the Gospel. Some have received it, but many deny it. I will prove to you through this chapter that Jesus made multiple appearances in the Old Testament even before He was born in the New Testament. By finding Jesus, you can utilize the prophetic gift using the scriptures with ease.

John the Apostle starts off in John 1:1 by saying, "In the beginning was the Word, and the Word was with God, and the Word was God." John was one of the closest disciples. He began to follow Jesus at a very young age. His Gospel reveals the divine side of God. In the other Gospels, they refer to Jesus' natural lineage. John is the only one who strictly deals with Jesus' divine lineage which only links His connection to God. In the very first verse, he starts it off by saying that God and the Word were the same. He also says that the Word was in the beginning. He then reiterates what he says, "The same was in the beginning with God" (John 1:2). He continues by further explaining what the Word did. In verse 14, he said the Word became flesh and dwelt among us. He is directly referring to Jesus.

John said Jesus was in the beginning. Yet, the name Jesus is not mentioned in the Old Testament, but the Word was. Let's reveal direct proof that Jesus was present in the Old Testament. This is not in chronological order.

1. When the three Hebrews were in the fiery furnace, Jesus showed up and walked in the fire with them. This is witnessed by the Babylonian King Nebuchadnezzar (Daniel 3:25). "He said the forth one looks like the Son of God."

2. Moses spoke with Jesus face to face. The same chapter says that he could not see the face of God and live, but he was able to see the face of Jesus. As a matter of fact, he spoke with Jesus face to face on several occasions. "And the Lord spake to Moses face to face, as a man speaketh unto his friend" (Exodus 33:11). How did he speak to God face to face and live if God said no man could see my face and live. The reason is that he was speaking with Jesus. Jesus has always been our connection to the Father. Through Jesus, we live and commune with God.

3. Jesus repeatedly visited Jeremiah. Jeremiah said, "Then the Word of the Lord came unto me, saying..." (Jeremiah 1:4). How can a word say anything? He meant Jesus came unto me saying. The name Jesus wasn't released at this time, but this was

Jesus who visited him. Listen to the Word. This was said several times in this book. Still don't believe it? Jesus is the Word. Jesus told Jeremiah, "Be not afraid of their faces: for I am with thee to deliver thee, saith the Lord. Then the Lord put forth his hand, and touched my mouth. And the Lord said unto me, behold, I have put my words in thy mouth (Jeremiah 1:9)." Jesus was the Word, and He was standing before Jeremiah. He placed His hands in his mouth, and Jesus said *I put my words in your mouth*. Jesus was the Word. When He put His hand in his mouth, His hand was the word. God, our Father, can't face us, and we still survive, so this was Jesus. How awesome is our God!

4. Jesus was the Voice of the Lord and the Word of God. No one can see the Father and live. Jesus has always been our direct link to Him. I will show you a few examples of Jesus' appearance in the Old Testament. First, we will begin with the first book of the Bible. In Genesis 3:8, it didn't just say that God walked in the midst of the garden. It said that the Voice of the Lord walked in the Garden. How can a voice walk? Too many people believe the Bible is just one big metaphor. When you believe this, you will miss Jesus every time. This was Jesus in the Garden. As a matter of fact, Jesus and the Holy Ghost were in the first chapter. Genesis 1:2 didn't say God moved upon the face of the waters, but it said that His Spirit did. In verse 3, Jesus makes His first appearance when "God said." The voice of God is Jesus. This is why John said that the same Jesus was in the BEGINNING (John 1:2).

5. Several prophets would use a statement saying the Voice of the Lord said, the Word of the Lord said,

and the hand of the Lord. These were all appearances by Jesus in the Old Testament. As I read the word, I take everything directly. According to theologians, there are only five poetic books of the Bible including Job, Psalms, Proverbs, Ecclesiastes, and the Song of Solomon. So, if you wish to believe the Bible is metaphoric, I will give the benefit of the doubt to these five books, but even in these five books, God is speaking directly. Isaiah would repeat, "The voice of the Lord came to me saying." After reading that repeatedly, I thought to myself, why would he say that? It should just be the Lord came unto me saying. God then revealed that it was Jesus because it was God's voice and word. A person says things, not a voice of a person. The voice was Jesus. The arm and hand of the Lord are also Jesus. He is our limb to God. Isaiah 53:1 says, "Who hath believed our report? And to whom is the arm of the Lord revealed." After this verse, the entire chapter is speaking of Jesus' coming and his visions of Jesus. The arm was Jesus. If you still don't believe me, here is my evidence. The word of God is Jesus according to John 1:1-14. Even the prophet Samuel would say that the "Word of the Lord came to me saying…" (1 Samuel 15:10). If you can agree with me on that, we can move forward in revelation. When you can see Jesus, it is prophecy.

6. Daniel and John had a vision of God with the skin of brass whose continence was bright as lightning and as the sun. This was Jesus in both cases. John says directly that it was Jesus. Daniel had the same experience and described Jesus the same way. But in the first case in Daniel chapter 10, Jesus wasn't even born yet. This is more evidence of Jesus in the Old Testament. Jesus comes and experiences humanity

by going through the entire process of being human, but He revealed Himself in His divine form in the Old Testament.

There are many more instances of Jesus appearing in the Old Testament, but these are just a few to show you. It troubles me when I hear Christians say that they don't even pay attention to the Old Testament. They are missing out on an amazing mystery of Jesus. Jesus came to fulfill the Old Testament, not do away with it (Matthew 5:17). When you can find Jesus, you are able to fulfill prophecy even more because prophecy is ultimately the testimony of Jesus. We must find Jesus when we prophesy.

Chapter 10

Utilizing the Word and Activation

I caution you to proceed to this chapter with caution. If you are not ready to start operating in the gift of prophecy, stop here. If you are ready to minister and understand Jesus in a newer way, you may proceed.

This is highly necessary to operate in the prophetic to benefit believers completely. Don't just give them an emotional high. God sent you to heal the sick, cast out devils, cleanse lepers, raise the dead, and prophesy (Matthew 10). Do you have issues with cursing, hatred, racism, lesbianism, homosexuality, drugs, alcoholism, fighting, stealing, murder, witchcraft, lying, gossip, extortion, pornography, or any bad habits that will separate you from God (1 Corinthians 6:9-11)? If you do and you are serious about God's work, give it up. I will stand with you and agree that these spirits of sin be removed. As I wrote this, I prayed for you. If you need deliverance, it is right here.

Touch this spot.

As I wrote this, I prayed over it and laid my hand on it. Hold your hand here for 1 minute. Any spirits inside of you that have caused you to sin will be removed. This will take away the taste you have for the sin that has beset you. After you touch this, you will have to give up habits, and you will lose the taste for it. Some of you will wait to have sex again until you are married. You will stop talking with people that make you fall. The only way it will return is if you purposely go back. I pray you don't but if you do return here and touch where my hand has been, you will be delivered.

I want you to stop what you are doing now and reflect on your life. Anything that doesn't align with God's righteousness must be removed. We can't allow things to get in the way of Jesus and His anointing. Elisha wasn't given leave to even tell his parents goodbye when he accepted the calling (1 Kings 19:19-21). What about telling our sins, bad habits, and people who separate us from God goodbye? As a prophet, you must be willing to sacrifice. Isaiah encountered God, and he wanted to remove his cursing issue (Isaiah 6). God wants to use you so badly, but too many people love their habits more than Jesus. So, if you are genuinely willing to work for Jesus, let's give it up and be renewed.

As you are reading this, God is opening your eyes to see the spirit realm. Too many people don't want to see what's going on. With the gift of discernment, you can see spirits and God. God is light. The enemy is the ruler of darkness. When there is spiritual darkness, it can be seen if you have the gift of discernment. This is why Paul said we don't battle against flesh and blood but unseen powers and principalities. Then he said rulers of darkness. God is light, and Satan rules darkness. The darkness has no power against light at all unless it has darkness (Ephesians 6:12.) Jesus is light, and there is no darkness in Him.

There are times I pray in the dark, and when I have touched heaven in my prayer time, the entire room lights up. I can see the light because the Lord gave me discernment. From now on, you will be able to identify light and darkness in the spirit realm.

Touch here to activate.

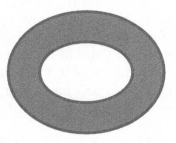

Jesus gave us power over darkness and unclean spirits. Jesus said I give you power to tread over scorpions, serpents, and over all the power of the enemy. Jesus said, "Nothing shall by any means hurt you" (Luke 10:19). There is nothing that can hurt you in any way possible when you fully operate in the Spirit because Jesus made it into a law when He said, "Touch not my anointed and do my prophet no harm (Psalm 105:15)." When we see darkness, it must be removed. If the person has given you access to be delivered, you have the power to set them free.

Demons must be cast out. When casting demons out, you must do more than say Jesus' name. If you don't have the authority and the virtue of Christ inside of you, saying Jesus' name may not do anything. This is how two men got beaten up by demons in Acts 19:13-16. These vagabond exorcists tried to cast out an evil spirit. They attempted by saying, "We cast you out in Jesus name of whom Paul preaches." The demon responded by saying we know Jesus and Paul but who are you? Then the demon-possessed man overpowered and inflicted injuries on them. So, using the name of Jesus isn't all that is needed. We need His virtue, principles, and power (Acts 19:13-16, Luke 8:28-31, and Mark 5).

As mentioned in earlier chapters; demons can actually say Jesus' name. Demons also worship, and they fear and tremble. Saying Jesus' name isn't enough. We must use His word and have authority. If we are wrapped in sin, we don't have authority. If we don't know what Jesus said, we don't have authority. We must use His word against them.

Most of the time, when I cast demons out, I use God's Word, and I let the devil know who I am in relation to Jesus. Jesus gave me authority over demons. Demons fear and tremble because of who Jesus made me to be. I have power over demons, and I can torment them. My position in Jesus and the power that He gave me is just as important as knowing and saying His name.

When people come to you for prayer in healing or deliverance, do it immediately. They came to you and if you have been given the ability to do it, then do it. They will receive it and be healed. The only time you don't do it is if God tells you not to. There have been people that I've prayed for, and Jesus healed them of cancers, blindness, paralysis, and other things. Yet, there have been times when individuals didn't want their healing as much as I did. There has been proof from doctors that individuals have been healed in Jesus Christ Ministry services, but there are people that didn't want to be healed. We are cleared to fully go to those whose faith is ready to receive a miracle. As freely as we've received our healing, freely give (Matthews 10:8). When there are those who don't want their healing or they are not willing to follow God's directions, we may not have full access to deliver them. I said *may not* because there are times when God takes over. Allow them to come to you. In order for that, Jesus has to be seen in you.

There are also times when God may not have you to deliver someone. There have been instances when God has told me to refrain from speaking deliverance and healing. That person may have done something wrong, or God is trying to get a point across. If I were to intervene, I might interrupt what God is trying to do. This has happened to me on multiple occasions. I've had loved ones that I wanted to see recover, but God told me not to speak healing on them. We cannot get in God's way. We can intercede, but we cannot go against God's order.

There was one guy who was following our ministry, and my staff and I got comfortable with him. He came to me and asked for prayer because he was going through some stuff. As I was in my prayer room, about to pray for him, the Lord stopped me and said I should not pray for him. I was stunned because I never heard that before, at that time. He sent me to Jeremiah 7:16. He said do not pray for him because he was not living right and God was doing something. I asked God, why? He said the man was practicing homosexuality and that God wanted him to get his house in order. God told me to tell him that he has three months to set his life in order and if it isn't by then, He will send judgment. The man didn't like this response. Three months later, he contacted me and told me that he was undergoing the judgment because he didn't follow direction. So, we must be keen on listening to God when we pray for people.

When they come to you, immediately discern what is going on. Find Jesus and locate the darkness that needs to be removed. In many cases of sickness, there is a spiritual infirmity that can be healed. What we have to do is to command that spirit to leave and allow Jesus to come in. In the next volume, we will go into detail about healing.

There was a lady who was coming to our church for years in a walker. The doctors had no idea why she couldn't walk right. CAT scans and x-rays showed nothing abnormal. Those doctors couldn't see in the spirit though. Every Sunday, we would pray for her and believed Jesus would heal her. She continued to barely walk out of church using her walker. When God revealed the spirit realm to me, it was almost suddenly that my ministry went to another level with healing. After I finished preaching, the Lord had me to open my eyes, and I saw a demon sitting on her hip. One of the other ministers caught hold of this revelation in my sermon. She began to cast spirits out of people who came up for prayer. The first lady that came up was delivered. As the minister prayed for her, she commanded the spirit to leave, and I saw it leave so quickly that as it left it hit my shoulder. I then called for the lady who couldn't walk and as I looked at that spirit on her hip. I commanded it to leave. I then told her to get up and run around the church. She leaped to her feet and ran around the church and immediately received her healing.

I said all of that because we need to identify spirits and stop befriending them. When we see them, we cast them out! After we cast them out, we must have the people to receive Jesus. The virtue on the inside of us fills them with Jesus as we touch them. This is how the woman with the issue of blood was healed. Jesus felt virtue taken out of Him when she touched Him in faith. We must get the people to activate their faith when they come to us and fill them with Jesus. If we don't have virtue in us, they may be filled emotionally by what we see, but the healing that is needed comes with the virtue. Virtuousness is purity, righteousness, and the love of Jesus. If we lack these things, we can easily impart more pain to them.

Before God gave me my deliverance ministry, I was sick while I was out of town. A preacher who was known to be a prophet began to pray for me. As he prayed for me, I started to get sicker, and I had to be rushed to the hospital. I heard other people who I was close to say the same thing happened to them. When I grew up, I learned that preacher that prayed for me was sleeping with other women around town even though he was married. Then I realized he had no virtue in order to deliver my sickness. Believe it or not, there are preachers causing harm to God's pasture just like this.

When we have the authority of Jesus on us, spirits are afraid. When Jesus would show up on the scene, demons would run to Him, begging Him not to torment them or send them to the abyss. We have the power to torment spirits. If we wanted to, we could have a spirit cut in pieces and thrown at the bottom of the Red Sea. We have the authority from Jesus. When you identify a spirit, we must ATTACK!!! You can command that spirit to leave that vessel and light it on fire from Hell. We must command the spirit to leave and place it somewhere. The best place to send them is Hell. The only way that spirit can come back is if that vessel goes back to the sin that the spirit controls. He is then released to cause torment on that vessel once more. Jesus even said it in Matthew 12:43-45. When a spirit is cast out of a person, they go around looking for rest. Finding none, they go back to the person they inhabited and bring several other spirits with him and the state of that person is worse than the beginning.

If you remember just a few paragraphs before, there was a woman healed in our church from being crippled because there was a demon on her hip. The Lord told me to tell her to throw her cane away and not return to the sin that caused that spirit to fall on her. If she didn't, she would end up in a wheelchair. I left town for a few months, and I came back. She was in a wheelchair. I knew this was an act of God. I was going to leave it alone because it was something that

God pronounced on her because of disobedience. I asked her if she followed my directions by throwing the cane and walker away. I was moved with compassion then. I told her again to throw away her cane along with the wheelchair and she will sustain her healing. As I prayed, she got up and ran around the church. She still decided to keep her cane and wheelchair. The following month, the spirit returned to her, and she was bound to the wheelchair ever since. This is a serious spirit world. We must be serious about Jesus.

We must then give Godly instructions to the individuals. This is where a lot of things go wrong in prophecy. We cannot mix it with our own emotion and personal opinion. It has to be Jesus' principles. If you use Jesus, you will never go wrong.

For us to see and hear Jesus, we must get still. Concentrate and focus on Jesus. He will soon start moving. There are times when I sing a song of thanks and follow it with a song of love to Him. From that point, I can inquire of Him. This is why Holy solemnness is necessary.

So, as an outline for Volume One of *Understanding and Maximizing the Gifts of Prophecy*, you must:

A. Be cleansed
B. Give thanks and worship
C. Reach holy solemnness
D. Allow God's Word to be spoken
E. Have your virtue and with Jesus' authority, attack demons
F. Replace that spirit with Jesus and make sure that person is filled up
G. Leave Godly instructions

The gift of prophecy is a gift from God. Through Jesus, we can think and even speak things into existence, alter reality, control the weather, see past and future events, heal diseases, cause diseases, and even speak life. We must be connected to Jesus to fully function at our maximum potential. Without Jesus, our gift is meaningless. Use your gift wisely and with Jesus at all times.

About Dr. Levy Q. Barnes, Jr.

Dr. Levy Q. Barnes Jr. received his prophetic calling from God before he was born when a prophet prophesied that his mother and father were expecting a prophet son when they didn't even realize that his mother was pregnant. He began seeing visions at the age of 3 and 11, he started preaching the Gospel of Jesus Christ. He was ordained as a minister at the age of 16, an elder at the age of 21, and a bishop at the age of 28. He received his Bachelors of Science in Biology, Masters in Divinity, and Doctorate in Philosophy with a concentration in Christian Counseling. Even though he is formally educated, the mass of his knowledge came from spending hours daily with Jesus in prayer and studying on his own.

Currently, he is the television host of "Your Miracle," a Christian Recording Artist, an author, an inventor, the CEO of Q. Productions LLC, and he is also the Bishop of Jesus Christ Ministries, Bethel Temple of Deliverance, Christ Temple of Deliverance, and Jesus

Never Fails Love and Fellowship Church. His passion is sharing the mysteries of Jesus Christ, performing miracles, educating, and empowering believers. He holds Prophecy Conferences, Nights of Worship, and Miracle Services to accomplish this. If you would like to be a part of this world-changing ministry go to www.drlevy.info to experience his ministry in person.

To send correspondence or donations, mail them to

P.O. Box 1467
Groves, TX 77619

Made in United States
North Haven, CT
23 September 2022

24462841R00061